Shakespeare's *Unruly* Women

Shakespeare's *Unruly* Women

Georgianna Ziegler
with Frances E. Dolan and Jeanne Addison Roberts

The Folger Shakespeare Library
Washington, D.C., 1997

Distributed by
University of Washington Press
Seattle and London

This volume has been published in conjunction
with the exhibition *Shakespeare's Unruly Women*,
presented at the Folger Shakespeare Library,
Washington, D.C., from February 18 through
August 9, 1997.

The exhibition and the catalogue have been
funded by The Winton and Carolyn Blount
Exhibitions Fund and the Andrew W. Mellon
Publications Endowment of the Folger Library.

Distributed by University of Washington Press,
Seattle and London
ISBN 0-295-97629-2

Photographs by Julie Ainsworth.

Cover illustration:
Kenny Meadows (1790–1874), Lady Macbeth,
engraving by W. H. Mote (original 1848).

Frontispiece:
Ada Rehan (1860–1916) as Kate in The Taming
of the Shrew, *photograph (c.1887).*

Table of Contents

Foreword

"Unruly women," "outlaws," "the female Wild," "the Other": these are some of the provocative terms used by feminist critics of Shakespeare in recent years to refer to the heroines, both on the page and transported to the stage by actresses with ever more "clamorous voices." Such scholars have helped us to take a fresh look at the heroines in an era in which we are re-evaluating the position of women within our own society.

The curator of this exhibition and her collaborators accept the concept of unruliness, but they also re-examine it from a very different perspective. Their attention is directed specifically to the representations of Shakespeare's women in the Victorian era, rather than on the Elizabethan stage. Dr. Georgianna Ziegler, the Louis B. Thalheimer Reference Librarian at the Folger, has culled from the Library's vast holdings a remarkably varied and illuminating array of books, manuscripts, and illustrations which provide a new understanding of how Shakespeare's heroines came to embody, reflect, and refract the values and assumptions of nineteenth-century English society. Dr. Ziegler has also contributed the Preface and four of the six sections of this catalogue. From them, and the accompanying essays by Professors Frances E. Dolan and Jeanne Addison Roberts, we learn that in the Victorian context the term "unruly" can only be used with some degree of irony: Shakespeare's feisty females were transvaluated—to the extent possible—into docile embodiments of domesticity, gentility, and deference. The precise modes by which Victorian ideals of female behavior came to be incorporated in particular actresses, editions, productions, and characters makes for an absorbing visual experience.

All three of the contributors to this catalogue —Dr. Ziegler and Professors Dolan and Roberts—deserve the Folger's warm thanks for presenting their impressive learning in unusually accessible and enjoyable prose. Professor William L. Pressly, Chairman of the Department of Art History at the University of Maryland, College Park, reviewed the chapter on Shakespearean illustration and made valuable suggestions. It is a particular pleasure to acknowledge the loan of a manuscript from the Horace Howard Furness Memorial Library, the distinguished Shakespearean collection of the University of Pennsylvania. Although they occasionally vied for the same treasures, Mr. Furness and the Folgers were friends, and so it is fitting that their association should continue through the institutions to which they bequeathed their collections.

Rachel Doggett, the Folger's Andrew W. Mellon Curator of Books, served as general editor of this catalogue. The Conservation Department, headed by J. Franklin Mowery assisted by Julie Biggs and Linda Hohneke prepared and installed the many objects included in the exhibition; Julie Ainsworth, Head of the Photography Department, photographed them for the catalogue. The staff of the Reading Rooms, headed by Betsy Walsh, took over some of Dr. Ziegler's responsibilities while she worked on the show, and Susan Sehulster managed to find just the right playbill to document an important performance at Covent Garden Theatre.

Finally, I am happy to acknowledge the support of two endowed funds which help to support aspects of the Folger's exhibition program, namely, The Winton and Carolyn Blount Exhibitions Fund and the Andrew W. Mellon Publications Endowment. To all these contributors, helpers, and donors, much thanks.

Werner Gundersheimer
Director

Preface

Georgianna Ziegler

This project began for me about eight or ten years ago when I first noticed several books illustrated with sets of portraits of Shakespeare's heroines. In some cases, the same set was used to illustrate different texts. That made me wonder how many of these pictures were made and why they were evidently so popular, especially in the nineteenth century. These questions, so apparently simple, led me on a fascinating journey into the world of the Victorians—their idealization of Shakespeare and of their Queen, their moral and physical construction of womanhood, their interest in physiognomy, and the development of a large middle-class market for printed materials and for works of art. All of these strands of inquiry proved important for understanding why, during that particular time, the interest in Shakespeare's heroines was so keen.

A female ruler who came to the throne as a lovely young woman, matured into copious motherhood, and endured a long and respected widowhood appealed to the imagination of a nation that enjoyed economic well-being at home and was expanding its influence over the world to create the greatest empire since the Romans. Queen Victoria was a mother both physically and metaphorically. She and her consort, the German Prince Albert of Saxe-Coburg-Gotha, produced nine children who married into many of the royal houses of Europe. As Head of State, the Queen was also depicted as a mother to the millions of persons who populated her vast empire. During her reign, the British middle class expanded, great interest was taken in the moral and educational training of young women, many more women began to publish their writings, actresses gained a degree of respectability they had not enjoyed before, and toward the end of the century, women began to agitate for suffrage and for entrée to university degrees.

The nineteenth century also saw a new fascination with Shakespeare, in England as well as in Germany, France, and America. The century produced major editions of Shakespeare's works, including the first edited by a woman, Mary Cowden Clarke, and innumerable works of art influenced by Shakespeare's plays. It gave rise to a new generation of Shakespeare critics and antiquarians, as well as to a thriving theatrical business which sent actors from England, America, and the Continent traveling and performing in each other's countries. The combination of Shakespeare and well-known stage personalities encouraged a kind of popular culture that we recognize today: illustrated newspaper and magazine articles, sets of inexpensive pictures for framing, Staffordshire figurines, mugs, tiles, and those eminently collectible photographs called *cartes-de-visites*.

The exhibition created here draws on the rich resources in the Folger Shakespeare Library, some of which were purchased by Henry Clay and Emily Jordan Folger during the late Victorian period when they began their collection. It includes material from the late eighteenth and early twentieth centuries but focuses primarily on the ways in which Shakespeare's heroines were appropriated into the moral, literary, and theatrical cultures of the nineteenth century. The exhibition and catalogue begin with considerations of how Shakespeare became implicated in the fashioning of womanhood through both moral education and the production of sets of heroine pictures. They move on to consider specific heroines, focusing on the comedies of the 1590s and the great tragedies; then they round out the turn-of-the-century with a look at the new psychoanalytic criticism and commentary occasioned by the three-hundredth anniversary of Shakespeare's death in 1916 on the eve of America's participation in the First World War.

Two final essays in the catalogue deal with twentieth-century interpretations of the heroines following the feminist movement of the sixties and raise the question, "*Are* Shakespeare's heroines unruly?" The provocative nature of this query and title demands an explanation. We do not suggest that Shakespeare set out to create rebellious feminists in the modern sense of the term. It would be anachronistic to believe so, for Shakespeare wrote in an age that defined women's roles largely in a hierarchical, male-oriented social structure. Nevertheless, it is fascinating to see the variety of ways his heroines operate in, rebel against, attempt to rule, or are crushed by this structure. This exhibition seeks to examine the ways in which the Victorian period interpreted Shakespeare's characters according to their own notions of what it meant to be a woman.

Queen Victoria, Shakespeare, and the Ideal Woman

✳

THE EXHIBITION, PART I

✳

Georgianna Ziegler

Queen Victoria liked Shakespeare. She and Prince Albert sponsored theatrical performances at Windsor, then at the Princess's Theatre in London. These included seventy-six performances of Shakespeare, the favorite plays being *King John*, *Macbeth*, *Richard II*, *Richard III*, *Henry V*, *King Lear*, and *The Winter's Tale*, all of which the royal party saw several times.[1] It is surely no accident that Queen Victoria's reign, 1837–1901, corresponded to a heightened cult of womanhood which revealed itself in a focus on the heroines of that other idol of the period, Shakespeare. This cultural phenomenon produced editions of Shakespeare's plays designed for "chaste ears," and studies of the heroines, beginning with Anna Jameson's *Characteristics of Women* (1832 and published throughout the century), moving to Mary Cowden Clarke's *Girlhood of Shakespeare's Heroines* (1850–52), and ending with Helena Faucit Martin's *On Some of Shakespeare's Female Characters* (1880–84), dedicated to the Queen herself. The phenomenon also produced several series of "portraits" of the heroines, among them Charles Heath's *Gallery* (1836–37); his *Heroines* (1848, 1858); and the *Graphic Gallery of Shakespeare's Heroines* (1888). All of these books and pictures were designed for popular consumption in various formats during the nineteenth century. We shall look at the portraits and other artistic representations in another essay. Here I want to explore the Victorian cultural context that produced the linking of Shakespeare with female morality.

From the eighteenth century on, girls and young women were encouraged to read Shakespeare as a way of improving the mind, but they were also provided with essays and books about Shakespeare's heroines in order to improve their own characters. As early as

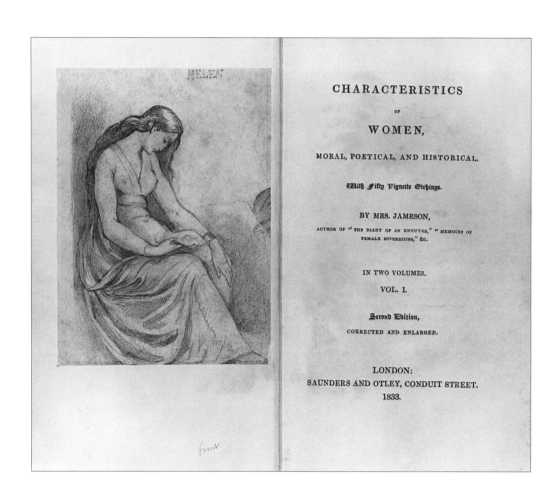

Title page opening from extra-illustrated edition
of Anna Jameson, Characteristics of Women,
2d ed. (London: Saunders and Otley, 1833)
showing original drawing by Jameson.

1793, Hester Chapone, the bluestocking, in *Letters on the Improvement of the Mind* addressed to her niece, advised that Shakespeare's "historical plays, if read in a series, will fix in your memory the reigns he has chosen, more durably than any other history."[2] In 1807, *Tales from Shakespeare* by Mary and Charles Lamb made the stories available to younger children. Years later the first woman to edit Shakespeare, Mary Cowden Clarke, remembered her introduction to the plays through these stories in a volume brought home by her father.[3] Also in 1807, Henrietta Bowdler published a four-volume expurgated edition of Shakespeare that, along with her brother's expansion of the work in 1818, was to become one of the most frequently published editions in the nineteenth century. The Preface to the Fourth Edition "assure[s] the parents and guardians of youth, that they may read the *Family Shakspeare* aloud in the mixed society of young persons of both sexes, *sans peur et sans reproche*."[4] A few years later in 1822, the Reverend J. R. Pitman brought out *The School-Shakspeare* which he dedicated to the great actress Sarah Siddons with admiring praise for her depiction of Shakespeare's heroines. He remarked that "the attention of young females, both in schools and in families, has, of late years, been carefully directed to the study of our English Classics," and that in his volume, "pupils may . . . peruse as much of Shakspeare, as is compatible with other objects of study. —Immoral language has been carefully excluded; so that taste may be cultivated, without offence to delicate and religious feelings."[5]

The nineteenth century saw the publication of hundreds of scholarly editions of Shakespeare, but the interest in expurgated editions for family consumption never abated. In 1876 Henry Cundell produced *The Boudoir Shakespeare*. The title, to our eyes, now seems humorously ironic, but Cundell, speaking of himself in the third person, was deadly serious in his purpose "to [expunge] such passages as, after the lapse of three centuries, might grate harshly on the ear; his aim being to strip the text of all that might wound a feminine sense of delicacy." The Preface continues:

He has often had to lament the exclusion, from the ordinary reading of our girls, of these noble works, by far the grandest monuments of the glory of English literature . . . . The work has been undertaken in no mawkish spirit, and it is hoped that the gentle reader will find nothing from which she may not 'with the safety of a pure blush in honour come off again,'. . . . If he is to be so happy as to evoke a kindly reception to the present venture, it must be on the ground of his honest, however humble, endeavour to present a selection from these incomparable dramas that shall be acceptable to Shakespeare's countrywomen on both sides of the Atlantic, to whom these volumes are inscribed with every feeling of respect and devotion . . . .[6]

Cundell designed his work for reading aloud in the privacy of the home (hence "boudoir," suggesting the intimate world of women), and there is ample evidence that both professional and amateur oral presentations of Shakespeare were popular middle-class activities in the nineteenth century. After she left the stage, Fanny Kemble established a career of giving public readings of the plays, while before she entered her successful acting career, Helena Faucit Martin read scenes from *The Winter's Tale* at school, "and never can I forget our getting them up to act as a surprise for our governess on her birthday."[7] But it was certainly not only actresses who read Shakespeare. Hannah Macaulay, sister of Thomas, the historian, talks about readings at home by their parents, including "Shakespeare (a great treat when my mother took the volume)." An even more typical middle-class mother, Martha Sharpe, writes of her daughter Molly: "I have promised to read a few of Shakespeare's historical Plays with her, in an Evening, when Aunt Kate is gone, & we are quite alone, as a great Treat."[8]

The Folger Library's copy of the Reverend Pitman's *School-Shakspeare* was owned by Ann M. Brown, who inscribed her name on the title page on January 31, 1823, and at least two other editions of the plays at the Folger were given as wedding presents to young women. One of these was presented by Mary Cowden Clarke to Minnie Chudleigh "with earnest wishes for her wedded happiness" in May 1893. What made Shakespeare's plays appropriate bridal gifts? In their Preface to this presentation volume (1875), Cowden Clarke and her husband, the editors, summarize the moral agenda that the nineteenth century brought to Shakespeare. "A poor lad, possessing no other book, might, on this single one, make himself a gentleman and a scholar. A poor girl, studying no other volume, might become a lady in heart and soul." Furthermore, Shakespeare is seen as creating standards for language, taste, and morals; "the inseparable happiness and preferableness of right, he never fails to inculcate by subtlest truth of demonstration."[9] Thus, whether consciously or unconsciously, Shakespeare's text is made comparable to a host of other books designed for the instruction and moral improvement of young women.

Among the most popular were those by Sarah Stickney Ellis. Her *Women of England*, appearing in 1838, was the first in an often-reproduced series, including *Daughters of*, *Wives of*, and *Mothers of England*, which set about to improve "the majority of the female population of Great Britain." When *Daughters of England* reached New York in 1842, a reviewer in *The Ladies' Companion* magazine called it "A work which cannot be too widely circulated in our country. Addressing itself . . . to the *middle* ranks of society only in Great Britain, it is admirably suited to the daughters, wives and mothers of a republican government."[10] Ellis asserts that "young ladies . . . of the present day, are distinguished by a morbid listlessness of mind and body, except when under the influence of stimulus, a constant pining for excitement, and an eagerness to escape from every thing [sic] like practical and individual duty."[11] Focusing on the large majority of women in the new middle class, Ellis strives to raise in them a sense of their moral responsibility as "domestic women," keepers of hearth and home. While Ellis does not deal specifically with Shakespeare, her emphasis on what constitutes Englishness finds its natural counterpart in the yoking of Shakespeare, considered that most English of all authors, with the moral development of England's women, as in the work of Jameson and others.

Ellis's construction of women as keepers of domestic tranquility and purveyors of national morality was reinforced by the Queen herself, who in 1844 wrote to her uncle King Leopold of Belgium, "They say no Sovereign was ever more loved than I am . . . and this because of our domestic home, the good example it presents."[12] The Queen was both the product of and the inspiration for the system of middle-class morality that made women queens of their own domestic realms.[13] This idealization of womanhood was epitomized mid-century in Coventry Patmore's four-part poem "The Angel in the House" (1854–1862), which sold 250,000 copies, and Ruskin's "Of Queens' Gardens," published in 1865 as part of his most popular work, *Of Sesame and Lilies*.

Patmore gave voice to images of women that were already established by mid-century.[14] His idealization of the middle-class wife as queen of her parlor domain was summarized with ironic bitterness in 1942 by Virginia Woolf, raised in a Victorian family, who felt she had to "kill off" this female icon before embarking on her own writing career:

. . . you may not know what I mean by the Angel in the House. I will describe her as shortly as I can. She was intensely sympathetic. She was immensely charming. She was utterly unselfish. She excelled in the difficult arts of family life. She sacrificed herself daily . . . . in short, she was so constituted that she never had a mind or a wish of her own, but preferred to sympathize always with the minds and wishes of others. Above all . . . she was pure . . . . In those days—the last of Queen Victoria—every house had its Angel.[15]

Like Patmore, Ruskin was also influenced by Victoria, the domestic Queen. But whereas Patmore's woman is more passive, living in the shadow of men, Ruskin says that each sex "completes the other."[16] He writes: "a woman has a personal work or duty, relating to her own home, and a public work or duty, which is also the expansion of that" — namely, "to assist in the ordering, in the comforting, and in the beautiful adornment of the state" (pp.164–165). Like Jameson, he finds his primary examples of womanhood in Shakespeare, who he says, "has no heroes; — he has only heroines" (p.116). "He represents them as infallibly faithful and wise counsellors, —incorruptibly just and pure examples,— strong always to sanctify, even when they cannot save" (p.121). In short, according to Ruskin's view, women in Shakespeare are acting as their real-life counterparts ought to act.

Ruskin may have been influenced by Anna Jameson's hugely popular work *Characteristics of Women, Moral, Poetical, and Historical*, published in 1832. Jameson wrote to support her family and turned out a number of publications on travel, literature, art, and women's issues. She numbered among her friends Fanny Kemble, Elizabeth Gaskell, Jane Carlisle, and George Eliot. *Characteristics of Women* went through at least four editions and about forty printings until 1911, and also appeared as *Shakespeare's Heroines* (thirty-three times from the 1870s to 1930) and as *Shakespeare's Female Characters*. The original title indicates that the book was conceived as being primarily "about" characteristics of women and only incidentally "about" Shakespeare's heroines. Through the character Alda in the introductory dialogue, Jameson professes to use Shakespeare as a teaching device "to illustrate the various modifications of which the female character is susceptible, with their causes and results," having found "that the education of women, as at present conducted, is founded in mistaken principles, and tends to increase fearfully the sum of misery and error in both sexes."[17] Jameson prefers examples from Shakespeare to those from history, for history is often not clear-cut, but Shakespeare's "characters combine history and real life; they are complete individuals, whose hearts and souls are laid open before us" (p.xix). The inspiration for Jameson's work then is not so much commentary on Shakespeare as a desire for the morally improving education of contemporary women.

Such was also the view of Mary Cowden Clarke, the first female editor of Shakespeare's works, whose immensely popular *Girlhood of Shakespeare's Heroines* (1851) was preceded by a series of articles published in *The Ladies' Companion* in 1849–50 and

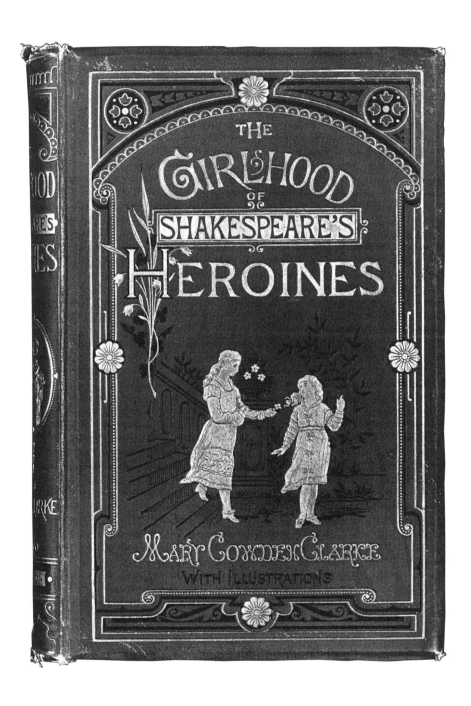

Ornamental binding of Mary Cowden Clarke,
The Girlhood of Shakespeare's Heroines, *new edition,*
condensed (London: Bickers and Son, 1893).

in 1854. In these articles she puts forth the view that woman should both see herself as she is in Shakespeare's heroines and also learn how to improve what she sees. Of all male authors, she writes, Shakespeare

has best asserted womanhood's rights . . . he has best admonished its failings . . . he has best proclaimed its capabilities, its magnanimity, its devotion, its enthusiasm, its fortitude, its patience, its endurance, its heroism, . . . he has best discerned and revealed its littlenesses, its foibles, its defects . . . its most evil aspects of depravity.[18]

When she writes her *Girlhood* series, her interest (though unstated) is on creating stories that will teach modern girls and their mothers how to identify and deal with a variety of behavioral and social problems, including sexuality. The "purifying" atmosphere of Shakespeare allows her to mention topics such as postpartum depression (Lady Macbeth's mother), unwanted advances and sexual abuse of children (Ophelia)—topics that would never be discussed openly in a Victorian home. Her study of the shrewish Kate's upbringing is a barely-disguised lesson in parenting: "instead of forming her child's disposition, and giving a wholesome tendency to such points of character, as might have grown into attractive qualities, with proper restriction and worthy culture," Kate's mother spent time on more trivial interests.[19] In such stories we are but one step away from the conduct books of a Mrs. Ellis or an Emily Shirreff.

The popularity of the books by Jameson and Cowden Clarke led to similar attempts such as *Shakespeare's Garden of Girls* (London, 1885) by M. Leigh Noel (Madeleine L. Elliott) and the American Henrietta Lee Palmer's *The Stratford Gallery; or the Shakspeare Sisterhood* (New York, 1859). Both women refer to the "sisterhood" of

Shakespeare's heroines; Leigh Noel says that "we can take their hands in honest faith and learn from them to appreciate more than ever nobility of character, singleness of purpose, and purity of ideal" (p.ii), while Palmer "claim[s] the right to speak of these, his Sisterhood, as one woman may justly speak of another . . . simply, naturally, sympathetically, as she may regard her fellow-women whom she meets from day to day" (Preface). All of these writers deal with Shakespeare's heroines as though they were real human beings with lives of their own outside the plays. But this fallacy was shared to a certain extent by some of the great Shakespeare scholars of the period such as Dowden, Heine, and Bradley, and was later recognized and countered by L.C. Knights in his famous essay, "How Many Children had Lady Macbeth?" (1946). A hundred years before Knights, however, Shakespeare's characters, like the characters in nineteenth-century novels, were read as reflecting real life. They were reconstructed by a different age in its own image, both by readers at home and by actors on stage.

It was from this latter perspective that Helena Faucit Martin wrote *On Some of Shakespeare's Female Characters*; first as letters to her friends, including the reformer Geraldine Jewsbury, Robert Browning, John Ruskin, and Alfred Lord Tennyson; then privately printed as little pamphlets and more publicly in *Blackwood's Magazine*; and finally published in one volume in 1885 with a dedication to Queen Victoria. The Queen, who was friendly toward Lady Martin and her husband, had approved of the essays from the beginning, writing to Sir Theodore Martin: "The Queen has much admired Lady Martin's characters of Ophelia and Desdemona. . . . Why should she not go on with all the Shakespearian female charac-

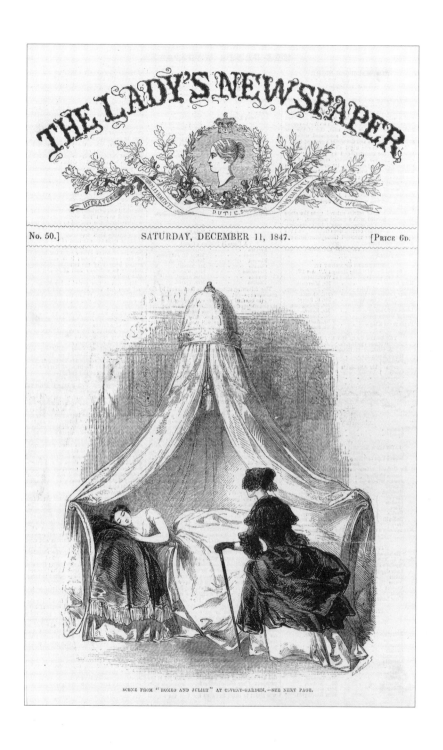

Front page of The Lady's Newspaper, *December 11, 1847,*
showing a scene from Romeo and Juliet
as performed at Covent Garden Theatre, London.

ters?"[20] When they were about to appear in book form, Her Majesty signaled her pleasure in having the volume dedicated to her. Though Martin bases her essays on her long experience in acting these heroines, her approach and purpose are similar to those of the other women writers we have seen. She writes of her empathy with the heroines: "I have, as it were, thought their thoughts and spoken their words straight from my own living heart and mind."[21] "My best reward" she continues, "would be, that my sister-women should give me, in return, the happiness of thinking that I have helped them, if ever so little, to appreciate more deeply, and to love with a love akin to my own, these sweet and noble representatives of our sex . . ." (p.viii).

Once again appears the word "sister." Long before a feminist sisterhood was born in the 1960s, nineteenth-century women writers appealed to an audience of fellow women among whom they expected to find sympathetic readers. The Queen was also a part of this sisterhood that included the fictional women of Shakespeare. The front page of *The Lady's Newspaper* for December 11, 1847, presents iconographically the conjunction of these social constructs: queen, heroines, sisterhood. A profile of the young Victoria graces the magazine's masthead, along with a motto that both advertises the magazine's offerings and suggests the proper interests for its female readership: "Literature Accomplishments Duties Amusements News." Beneath the masthead, a black-and-white line drawing shows a young woman in a canopied bed, with an older woman, whose face we cannot see, in black Victorian dress by her side. The young woman's face is that of the young Victoria above; the woman in black resembles the widow Victoria was to become. Without the caption beneath, we would not guess that these two women are Juliet and her mother, Lady Capulet, in a performance of scenes from Shakespeare's plays at Covent Garden Theatre. Here is the Queen in company *with* Shakespeare's heroines and represented as one *of* them in a periodical read by thousands of middle-class Englishwomen, who, if they were not really "angels in the house," at least constituted a Victorian sisterhood.

Notes

1   Theatrical performances for the Queen are listed in George Rowell, *Queen Victoria Goes to the Theatre* (London: Paul Elek, 1978), Appendix.

2   Hester Chapone, *Letters on the Improvement of the Mind, Addressed to a Young Lady*, "New edition" 2 vols. (New York: T. Allen, 1793), II:111.

3   Mary Cowden Clarke, Manuscript "Passage, extracted from the 'Preface' of the New York Edition, by Mary Cowden Clarke," tipped into the front of the Folger Library copy of *The Works of William Shakespeare*, edited by Charles and Mary Cowden Clarke, "The Leicester Square Edition" (London: Bickers & Son, 1875).

4   Thomas Bowdler, "Preface to the Fourth Edition," in *The Family Shakspeare* (London: Longman, Green, et al, 1863), v. The Folger Library's copy of this volume bears the inscription: "Florence Cope from her Papa, Christmas 1863."

5 J. R. Pitman, "Advertisement" in *The School-Shakspeare* (London: J. F. Dove for C. Rice, 1822).

6 Henry Cundell, "Preface" in *The Boudoir Shakespeare: Carefully Prepared for Reading Aloud* (London: Sampson Low, Marston, et al, 1876), 3–4, 6.

7 Helena Faucit, Lady Martin, quoted in Sir Theodore Martin, *Helena Faucit (Lady Martin)* (Edinburgh and London: William Blackwood and Sons, 1900), 4.

8 Both references quoted in Jenny Uglow, *Elizabeth Gaskell: A Habit of Stories* (New York: Farrar Straus Giroux, 1993), 41, 42. Uglow notes, "Interesting that in both families it is a great treat when the mother reads the Bard" (42).

9 Charles and Mary Cowden Clarke, "Preface" in *The Works of William Shakespeare* (London: Bickers & Son, 1875), i–ii.

10 *The Ladies' Companion: A Monthly Magazine Embracing Every Department of Literature*, 17 (New York: May 1842), 67.

11 Sarah Stickney Ellis, *The Women of England* (London: Fischer, 1839), 12.

12 Quoted in Duncan Crowe, *The Victorian Woman* (London: George Allen & Unwin, 1971), 51.

13 See Crowe, 51 and Elizabeth Langland, *Nobody's Angels: Middle-Class Women and Domestic Ideology in Victorian Culture* (Ithaca: Cornell University Press, 1995), Chapter 3.

14 Langland, 70.

15 Virginia Woolf, "Professions for Women," in *The Death of the Moth and other Essays* (London: Hogarth Press, 1942), 150.

16 John Ruskin, "Of Queens' Gardens," in *Sesame and Lilies* (New York: Charles E. Merrill, 1891), 135. All references to Ruskin are to this edition.

17 Anna Jameson, *Characteristics of Women, Moral, Poetical, and Historical* (Boston: Phillips, Sampson, and Company, 1854), xii–xiii. All references to Jameson are to this edition.

18 Quoted in Richard Altick, *The Cowden Clarkes* (London: Oxford University Press, 1948), 137.

19 Mary Cowden Clarke, Tale VII. "Katharina and Bianca; the Shrew, and the Demure," in *The Girlhood of Shakespeare's Heroines*, 5 vols. (New York: A. C. Armstrong and Son, 1891), III: 20.

20 Quoted in Sir Theodore Martin, 369.

21 Helena Faucit, Lady Martin, *On Some of Shakespeare's Female Characters*, 5th ed. (Edinburgh and London: William Blackwood and Sons, 1893), viii.

The Exhibition—Part I

✳ Mary Cowden Clarke, *The Girlhood of Shakespeare's Heroines*, new edition, condensed by her sister, Sabilla Novello (London: Bickers and Son, 1893). This volume is packaged as a gift book, showing on its ornate binding an older girl come to read it to her younger sister.

✳ M. Leigh Noel (Madeleine L. Elliott), *Shakspeare's Garden of Girls* (London: Remington & Co., 1885).

✳ *The Girl's Own Paper*, July 1887 (London: The "Leisure Hour" Office). This issue of a magazine for young women contains an article by Mary Cowden Clarke, "Shakespeare as the Girl's Friend," in which she writes: "To the young girl, emerging from childhood and taking her first step into the more active and self-dependent career of woman-life, Shakespeare's vital precepts and models render him essentially a helping friend."

✳ Helena Faucit, Lady Martin, Manuscript essay on "Ophelia" to Geraldine Jewsbury (c.1880). Horace Howard Furness Memorial Library, Manuscript Collection. University of Pennsylvania. This essay on Ophelia was written by Lady Martin at the request of her friend, the reformer and writer Geraldine Jewsbury. Martin says, "Ophelia was one of the pet dreams of my girlhood—partly, perhaps, from the mystery of her madness." Much in the style of Mary Cowden Clarke, she had imagined a whole previous life for Ophelia which helped her to mold the character when she acted her on stage in Paris for the first time with William Charles Macready as Hamlet.

✳ Helena Faucit, Lady Martin, *On Ophelia and Portia* (London: For strictly Private Circulation, 1880).

✳ Henrietta Lee Palmer, *The Stratford Gallery; or the Shakspeare Sisterhood: Comprising Forty-Five Ideal Portraits* (New York: D. Appleton and Company, 1859). Illustrated with the first set of Heath engravings.

✳ Anna Jameson, *Characteristics of Women, Moral, Poetical, and Historical*. With fifty Vignette Etchings. 2 vols. Second edition (London: Saunders and Otley, 1833). The Folger copy contains the original drawings by Jameson, along with the final etchings.

Shakespeare's Beauties Illustrated

*

THE EXHIBITION, PART II

*

Georgianna Ziegler

Picture the Victorian parlor, that crowded room overflowing with horsehair sofas, shawl-covered piano, perhaps a stuffed bird under glass, certainly a multitude of lace doilies and china brick-a-brack, dark engravings on the walls, and copies of the Bible, Shakespeare, a ladies' annual, and several picture books on the many tables. Here the family gathered to read and sew in the evenings or to entertain friends and gentleman callers. Lacking our modern enticements—television, computer games, and movies—the Victorians turned to reading aloud and looking at pictures for entertainment. The rapidly developing printing industry took advantage of this growing middle-class appetite and churned out newspapers, magazines, serial novels, decorative gift-book annuals, individual engravings, and "beauties" books, those collections of pictures of women from real life or literature offered with appropriate quotations.

Shakespeare, the great national poet, provided inspiration for at least some of these. His plays had already formed the subject matter for Josiah Boydell's attempt, at the end of the previous century, to create a school of English history painting by commissioning a whole gallery of oil paintings on Shakespearean themes. These works by the likes of Fuseli, West, Smirke, Kauffman and Westall were the predecessors to a host of nineteenth-century Shakespearean paintings, including a number featuring the heroines by women artists such as Fanny Corbaux, Lucy Madox Brown, Margaret Gillies, Emma Sandys and Rebecca Solomon.[1]

Since only the upper classes or newly-rich industrialists could afford to buy the paintings themselves, the large middle-class market was fed by engraved reproductions, sold as sets in portfolios ready for framing,

OTHELLO & DESDEMONA.

To Joseph Marsland, Esq.ᵉ Manchester
This print from the Original Picture in his Collection is respectfully dedicated by
The Publishers

Henry Liverseege (1803–1832), Othello & Desdemona,
painting, engraved by J.E. Coombs (Manchester, n.d.).
The painting was owned by Joseph Marsland, Esq.,
of Manchester.

or issued in magazines or gift books.[2] Fanny Kemble, the actress, remembered that as a child she had visited the drawing-room of friends where "tall china jars of pot-pourri filled the air with a mixed fragrance of roses and . . . plum-pudding, and where hung a picture, the contemplation of which more than once moved me to tears, after I had been given to understand that the princely personage and fair-headed baby in a boat in the midst of a hideous black sea . . . were Prospero, the good Duke of Milan, and his poor little princess daughter, Miranda, cast forth by wicked relations to be drowned."[3] Many years later Kemble excelled in giving public readings of *The Tempest*, the play that had so caught her fancy through this picture.

Alongside the reproductions of these works of "fine" art flourished several more "popular" varieties of art that drew their inspiration directly from Shakespeare's heroines, imagined either as actresses who portrayed them on stage or as types of female beauty. There always seems to be a market for pictures of actresses, and the eighteenth and nineteenth centuries were no exception. Sarah Siddons, leading tragic actress of her day, was painted by Gainsborough, Reynolds, and Westall, but she was also depicted as Lady Macbeth in numerous engravings used singly or as book illustrations, and even in chess pieces. Her contemporary, Dorothy Jordan, the leading comic actress, could find her face in miniature on a box lid, or her depiction of Rosalind in an engraving based on her celebrated stage presentation of that "breeches" role. Jane Lessingham's Ophelia was captured forever on a Liverpool delft tile, while Charlotte and Susan Cushman, playing Romeo and Juliet, were memorialized in a Staffordshire china figurine. Engravings of costumed actors and actresses,

singly or in sets, colored or in black-and-white, were popular throughout the period. When photography finally appeared in the later nineteenth century, *cartes-de-visites* with the likes of Sarah Bernhardt as Hamlet or Ellen Terry as Ophelia could be collected like baseball cards.

Actresses depicting Shakespeare's heroines were not necessarily beauties—one need only look at Eleanor Glynn or Charlotte Cushman as Lady Macbeth—but the market for lovely faces was supplied through another source: the sets of engravings put out as "Galleries" of Shakespeare's heroines. The first of these, produced by the engraver and illustrator Charles Heath, appeared in 1836–37, the first year of Victoria's reign. A series of booklets in pink paper wrappers offered forty-five pictures of Shakespeare's heroines interleaved with brief quotations from the plays. These inexpensive paperbacks directed to a middle-class audience became so popular that the images were copied to illustrate books about the heroines in France (*Galerie des Femmes de Shakspeare*, 1840s), Germany (Heinrich Heine's *Shakespeare's Mädchen und Frauen*, 1839), and America (Henrietta Lee Palmer's *The Stratford Gallery; or the Shakespeare Sisterhood*, 1859). Heath capitalized on their success by issuing a second set of engravings in 1848 that went through five editions until 1883, adding three more portraits to the original forty-five. They were based on paintings of the heroines by some of the most popular Victorian artists: Wright, Frith, Egg, Meadows, Hayter, Corbould, and Johnston. Eventually they were also reproduced as illustrations to the Routledge 1859 and Appleton 1860 editions of Shakespeare's Works, and to Anna Jameson's *Characteristics of Women* in British and American editions, where they are sometimes in color.

Kenny Meadows (1790–1874), Cleopatra,
colored engraving by H. Cook from Charles Heath,
The Shakspeare Gallery: Containing the Principal
Female Characters in the Plays of the Great Poet
(London: Charles Tilt, c.1836).

Kenny Meadows (1790–1874), Cleopatra,
colored engraving by J. Brown from Anna Jameson,
Characteristics of Women *(New York: John Wiley, 1850).*
From the second Heath Heroines, *originally published 1848.*

In the first Heath gallery, the heroines are shown as three-quarter figures dressed in period costumes, usually against a suggested background: Joan of Arc on a battlefield, Rosalind in a wooded place, Titania in a flowery bower. More attempt is made to suggest costume in the Roman and history plays than in the comedies, which are generically Victorian/Elizabethan, making it difficult to tell Julia from Rosalind or Silvia from Beatrice or Portia. In the second set, the figures are larger—Mrs. Ford has her letter, Helena a walking staff and straw hat, Lady Macbeth a dagger, and Titania her flowers, but again most of the heroines are not particularly distinguished by prop or costume. The emphasis instead is on the face, for a central belief in Victorian literature and art was "that the physical type indicates the moral."[4]

A similar focus exists in a third set, *The Beauties of Shakspere*, issued in the 1840s or 50s with fifty-two engravings drawn by W. G. Standfast. His thesis is that every woman created by Shakespeare "is a distinct representative of a class, whose prototype is ever to be found in mental or physical life, and forms a striking contrast to her opposite." They "typify every phase of life among the 'gentle sex' from the most repulsive to the most endearing." Standfast's black-and-white portraits face each other in pairs; the emphasis is on the head with a few attributes or other characters sketched in as decorative motif below. The pairings are not by play and set up some odd juxtapositions that are probably meant to be thought-provoking: for example Margaret of Anjou and Perdita; Portia (*Merchant*) and Audrey; Lady Macduff and Cordelia; Miranda and Ophelia. The faces are so stereotyped and so Victorian in their appearance, however, that one of their main functions must be to encourage young women to read their own vices and virtues in them.

Physiognomy, the determination of moral character by observing facial features, was all the rage. It provided a gendered code through which both class and character could be distinguished by facial attributes. In 1848 one physiognomist wrote:

The energies and tastes of women are generally less intense than those of men; hence their characters appear less developed and exhibit greater uniformity. That their passions are stronger is undeniable, but these do not constitute character . . . . Their indexes are the eyes and mouth.[5]

Leigh Hunt, friend of Shelley and Keats, remarks on the accepted view of eye color in his essay "Criticism on Female Beauty" (published 1847): "Black eyes are thought the brightest, blue the most feminine, grey the keenest," but he adds his own belief that "it depends entirely on the spirit within."[6] He continues, "The shape of the head, including the face, is handsome in proportion as it inclines from round into oval" (p.193). As for the lips, their size was thought to indicate the degree of sensual appetite. Thin lips obviously suggest restraint; the rosebud mouth of so many heroines "compresses passion into fastidiousness"; while large lips signal voluptuousness. Uneven lips, usually the upper smaller and the lower one full, create a mouth which "is the most sensual of all, for following the physiognomical interpretation, it promises to give more enjoyment than it demands in return."[7]

Most of the Shakespeare heroines follow this code; in Heath's second series, Juliet, Perdita, Miranda, and Ophelia have the rosebud lips and sweet faces of Victorian girls daydreaming, while Portia the lawyer shows a fuller lower lip, and Rosalind with her hair cropped short looks out at us with humor in her eyes. As might be expected, Kate the Shrew, Lady Macbeth, and Margaret of Anjou have stormy brows. All of them, however, are presented as types of Victorian beauties.

The rage for collections of such "portraits" in Britain likely originated with "Sir Peter Lely's series of Windsor Beauties painted in oils for Anne Hyde, Duchess of York, in 1662–65 and Sir Godfrey Kneller's Hampton Court Beauties painted in the same medium for Mary II c.1691." [8] During the eighteenth century, following the model established by the Reverend James Granger, a craze developed for "grangerizing" books of biography or history—that is, adding a large number of portrait heads and other historic engravings to the text. Granger's system of organizing pictures according to social classes included "Class XI Ladies and others, of the Female Sex, according to their Rank, &c."[9] By the following century, books focusing only on portraits of women became popular. In 1814 the artist Anne Foldsome Mee completed, for King George IV, a set of portrait miniatures as a "Gallery of Beauties," some of which appeared in a two-volume set, *Portrait Gallery of Distinguished Females including Beauties of the Courts of George IV and William IV* (1833) (Lloyd, p.190). A rough count shows at least twelve different "beauties" titles between 1833 and 1857, not including the Shakespeare heroines.[10] These range from the *Female Portraits of the Court of Queen Victoria* (1839), to the literary beauties of Walter Scott, Byron, and the Irish poet Thomas Moore. In all of these books, as in the popular women's magazines of today, the emphasis is on the depiction of female beauty, however idealized. Neither the court ladies surrounding Victoria nor the exotic *guises* of Byron's heroines nor certainly the Victorian maidens masquerading as Shakespeare's heroines could provide realistic models for most of their audience; but then, neither can the slim, tall, youthful bodies of

our own fashion models. The so-called insipid quality of many of these pictures is again a social construct, based on expectations about beauty and ways of seeing which are different from our own but were just as powerful then as now in enforcing society's notion of what constitutes the feminine.

At the end of the century, in 1888, a fourth set of engravings appeared and marked a departure from the others in marketing techniques and in appearance. The *Graphic* magazine, a popular London publication with a circulation in the hundreds of thousands, commissioned a series of twenty-one paintings of Shakespeare's heroines by some of the leading artists of the day (including Laura Alma-Tadema, the only woman artist represented in any of these series) which they displayed in a London gallery. These paintings were reproduced as double-page centerfolds purchased with the magazine, but they were also sold in special large portfolio editions that could be viewed on a table or individually framed. Each picture was accompanied by a folded leaf containing a plot summary/commentary by the poet William Earnest Henley (these were also sold separately as a small book, presumably to be carried when walking around the gallery). In 1896 *The Graphic* also offered a smaller-sized set of colored engravings, suitable for framing, in small grey-board portfolios. About the size of the color reproductions sold at many museums today, they were obviously directed at a similar middle-class market.

The style of the portraits themselves has undergone a transformation. Some, such as Ophelia, Juliet, Portia, and Jessica are still variations on the classic nineteenth-century beauty, but others derive from a range of artistic models: Desdemona from Italian Renaissance painting, Anne Page and Mariana from Dutch seventeenth-century painting, and Isabella from the Pre-Raphaelites. A contemporary reviewer praised the set as "one of the most sumptuous and . . . most artistic publications that we have lately seen," and he singled out Leighton's Desdemona, "remarkable for the masterly treatment of the rich Venetian costume," and the "Oriental splendour" of Waterhouse's Cleopatra (*Graphic*, Feb. 2, 1889, 107). Indeed, J. W. Waterhouse's portrait of Cleopatra marks the end of an era. This splendid woman, gazing out from under dark sultry brows as she lounges easily on a leopard skin, has a *fin-de-siècle* air about her. Heath's Cleopatras of forty years earlier are stiff and restrained in their Victorian corsets. This Cleopatra's unsupported breasts lie suggestively beneath her loose white tunic; she invites and repels, commands admiration and respect. She is "My serpent of old Nile," as the accompanying quotation says, not a Victorian lady with pouting lips in "dress-up." This painting by Waterhouse looks not backward but forward to the loosening of garments and morality, and to the changes in women's roles that would come with the Edwardian period and the Great War. The New Woman has broken away from the Victorian enterprise that bound women and Shakespeare to a moral notion of British nationalism dominated for nearly a century by the ideology of a Queen.

Notes

1   These and other women artists inspired by literature are discussed by Pamela Gerrish Nunn in "Between Strong-Mindedness and Sentimentality: Women's Literary Painting," *Victorian Poetry*, 33 (1995), 425–447.

2   Richard Altick discusses the varied audience for Victorian art in *Paintings from Books: Art and Literature in Britain, 1760–1900* (Columbus: Ohio State University Press, 1985), Chapter 4, especially 73–77.

3   Frances Ann Kemble, *Records of a Girlhood*, 2d ed. (New York: Henry Holt and Co., 1879), 24–25.

4   Mary Cowling, *The Artist As Anthropologist: The Representation of Type and Character in Victorian Art* (Cambridge: Cambridge University Press, 1989), 113.

5   Eden Warwick, *Nasology* (1848), 108, quoted in Jeanne Fahnestock, "The Heroine of Irregular Features: Physiognomy and Conventions of Heroine Description," *Victorian Studies*, 24 (1981), 344. Queen Victoria herself came under the influence of these beliefs through Thomas Woolnoth, her physiognomist and engraver. See Cowling, 12.

6   Leigh Hunt, "Criticism on Female Beauty," in *Men, Women and Books: A Selection of Sketches, Essays, and Critical Memoirs* (London: T. Werner Laurie, 1943), 188.

7   Fahnestock, 342, 343.

8   Christopher Lloyd and Vanessa
    Remington, *Masterpieces in Little: Portrait
    Miniatures from the Collection of Her Maj-
    esty Queen Elizabeth II* (London: Royal
    Collection Enterprises, Ltd., 1996), 190.

9   Marcia Pointon, *Hanging the Head:
    Portraiture and Social Formation in
    Eighteenth-Century England* (New Haven
    and London: Yale University Press for
    The Paul Mellon Centre for Studies in
    British Art, 1993), 56.

10 For discussion of these "beauties" books
    see Basil Hunnisett, *Steel-engraved Book
    Illustration in England* (London: Scolar
    Press, 1980). Charles Heath contributed
    prominently to these series. In addition to
    his two Shakespeare sets, he produced
    Gems of Beauty, *Beauties of the Opera*,
    and *English Beauties*. Another predeces-
    sor to the sets of Shakespeare character
    portraits are the twelve engravings
    published by John Hamilton Mortimer
    (1741–1779) entitled, *Shakespeare's
    Characters: A Series of Heads* (London,
    1775–76), that included heads of Ophelia,
    Beatrice, and Cassandra.

The Exhibition—Part II

* *The Shakspeare Gallery, containing the Principal Female Characters in the Plays of the Great Poet* . . . engraved . . . under the direction . . . of Mr. Charles Heath (London: Charles Tilt, 1836). This is the prospectus for Heath's first collection of Shakespeare "beauties" portraits.

* Charles Heath, *The Shakspeare Gallery* (London: Charles Tilt, c.1836). The Folger copy is inscribed: "Betty Temple from her affectionate Brother William on her attaining her 22nd birthday 12th November 1846."

* *Galerie des Femmes de Shakspeare: collection de 45 Portraits* (Paris: L.-P. Dufour et Mulat, c.1840). This collection of portraits from the first Heath set is accompanied by short essays on each heroine; the one for Cleopatra is appropriately written by the unconventional novelist George Sand.

* *Les Femmes de Shakespeare: Quarante-Cinq Magnifiques Portraits.* La Vie de Shakespeare par M. De Pongerville; Étude sur le Même auteur par M. Villemain (Paris: Gallet, Braud et Cie, n.d.). Another more elaborate edition of the first Heath beauties with accompanying essays.

* *The Heroines of Shakspeare: comprising the Principal Female Characters in the Plays of the Great Poet.* Engraved in the Highest Style of Art, from Drawings by Eminent Artists. (London: The London Printing and Publishing Company, n.d.). This volume is illustrated with the second set of Shakespeare "beauties" produced by Charles Heath.

* W. G. Standfast, *The Beauties of Shakspere* (London: J. Dicks, n.d.). Standfast's book presents fifty-two engravings of the heroines with no text.

* *The Graphic Gallery of Shakespeare's Heroines. The Graphic* magazine, a popular London publication with a circulation in the hundreds of thousands, commissioned a series of twenty-one paintings of Shakespeare's heroines by some of the leading artists of the day, including both Laura Alma-Tadema, the only woman artist represented, and her husband Sir Lawrence. The paintings were displayed in a London gallery around 1888 and reproduced as double-page centerfolds purchased with the magazine. They were also sold in portfolio editions that could be viewed on a table or individually framed. The Folger Library has sets of both the larger black-and-white and smaller colored goupilgravures. A contemporary reviewer praised the set as "one of the most sumptuous and . . . most artistic publications that we have lately seen."

Edmund Blair Leighton, R.A. (1853–1922),
Olivia *from* The Graphic Gallery of Shakespeare's Heroines
(Printed in Paris by Goupil for Sampson Low, Marston
& Company, London, 1896).

Sir Samuel Luke Fildes, R.A. (1843–1927),
Jessica *from* The Graphic Gallery of Shakespeare's Heroines
(London, 1896).

Marcus Stone, R.A. (1840–1921),
Ophelia *from* The Graphic Gallery of Shakespeare's Heroines
(London, 1896).

Lady Laura Alma-Tadema (1852–1909),
Queen Katherine (Henry VIII) *from*
The Graphic Gallery of Shakespeare's Heroines
(London, 1896).

Philip Hermogenes Calderon, R.A. (1833–1898),
Juliet *from* The Graphic Gallery of Shakespeare's Heroines
(London, 1896).

John William Waterhouse, R.A. (1849–1917),
Cleopatra *from* The Graphic Gallery of Shakespeare's Heroines
(London, 1896).

Kenny Meadows (1790–1874),
Lady Macbeth, *engraving by W. H. Mote*
originally made for Charles Heath
(London, 1848).

Friedrich Brockmann (b. 1809),
Portia and Nerissa *(1849), oil painting.*

Thomas Francis Dicksee (1819–1895),
Anne Page *(1862), oil painting.*

William Heath (1795–1840),
Miss Walstein as Rosalind,
handcolored engraving
(London: T. Palser, June 18, 1815).

Handcolored "penny plain" print
of Mrs. H. Johnston as Rosalind in
'As You Like It' *(London: W. West*
at his Theatrical Print Warehouse,
March 20, 1813).

Nineteenth-century porcelain figurine
of Charlotte and Susan Cushman playing
Romeo and Juliet.

"She is to enter now": the Heroines in the Plays

*

THE EXHIBITION, PART III

*

Georgianna Ziegler

Juliet

✳

ROMEO AND JULIET 1595–96

"All Shakspeare's women, being essentially women, either love or have loved, or are capable of loving; but Juliet is love itself." Anna Jameson's remark in 1832 sets the tone for the nineteenth-century's view of Juliet as the young teenager, full of imagination and passion, given over to the thrill of her first love. Raised in the wealthy Capulet household, by parents who left her care to the Nurse, Juliet leads a sheltered life until she meets Romeo. Then her determination to marry this man from an enemy family leads her to resist her parents and strike out on her own. As M. Leigh Noel says of Juliet in 1885: "When a woman unites these two qualities—resolution and cunning—what is there she cannot effect?" Shakespeare's earliest tragedy "appeals to the most glowing imaginations and deepest feelings of youth."

Detail from John Hayter (1800–1891), Romeo and Juliet, *Act I, scene v, proof lithograph by W. Sharp, showing Fanny Kemble as Juliet and Mrs. Davenport as the Nurse in a production at Covent Garden, c. 1830.*

✳ William Shakspeare, *Romeo and Juliet: A Tragedy, In Five Acts . . . As now performed at the Theatres Royal, London* (London: John Cumberland, n.d.). Prompt copy belonging to Helen Faucit (later, Helena Faucit, Lady Martin) who signed her name on the title page and on the first page of text. When Faucit first tried to perform Juliet in 1833 at the age of sixteen at the theater in Richmond, Yorkshire, she was so nervous that she broke the glass vial of sleeping potion in her hand and almost fainted on stage. Three years later she returned to the role at Covent Garden Theatre and made it her own.

✳ Playbill, Theatre Royal, Covent Garden. *Romeo & Juliet*, Thursday, March 10th, 1836. This playbill advertises Helen Faucit's first professional appearance as Juliet, paired with the sixty-one-year-old Charles Kemble as Romeo.

✳ A mid-nineteenth-century drawing of Juliet that conveys the young woman's fear of taking the sleeping potion from the vial she holds tightly in her hand, much as the youthful Helen Faucit did on stage. This Juliet's features are typically

Victorian and bear an uncanny resemblance to John Tenniel's famous drawings for Lewis Carroll's *Alice's Adventures in Wonderland* (1865).

✳ Nathaniel Currier (1813–1888), *Romeo and Juliet, Act III, scene v*, colored lithograph (New York, c.1840). The stiff poses and stage-set surroundings suggest that Currier may be reproducing a scene from an American production of the play, possibly that with Charlotte Cushman as Romeo in Albany, New York (1837), which was enthusiastically received. Currier, of course, is best known for his partnership with James Merritt Ives in their lithographs of charming New England scenes.

✳ John Hayter (1800–1891), *Romeo and Juliet, Act I, scene v,* sketch and proof lithograph by W. Sharp showing Juliet and her Nurse. Hayter made a series of sketches based on Fanny Kemble's performance as Juliet, with Mrs. Davenport as the Nurse, at Covent Garden, c.1830. The sketches served as designs for a book of lithographs, *Sketches of Miss Fanny Kemble in the Character of Juliet* (London: Engleman, Graff, et al, Feb. 12, 1830), for which Anna Jameson wrote the text.

✳ George Dawe (1781–1829), Study for *Miss O'Neill as Juliet* (c.1816), oil painting. Eliza O'Neill (1791–1872) first performed Juliet in 1811 on the Dublin stage and was such a success that she was hired at Covent Garden in London, where she debuted in this role on October 6, 1814. William Hazlitt wrote of her: "Her excellence—unrivalled by any actress since Mrs. Siddons—consisted in truth of nature and force of passion." Dawe here captures her in a pensive mood, suggested

by Act II, scene ii, where Juliet dreams about Romeo on her balcony: "See where she leans her cheek upon her hand."

✳ Two scenes of *Romeo and Juliet* from news magazines indicate how the icons of Queen Victoria and Shakespeare informed each other during the nineteenth century. The cover of *The Lady's Newspaper* for December 11, 1847, shows the scene of Lady Capulet by Juliet's bed as performed at Covent Garden Theatre, but Juliet's features mirror the face of the young Victoria on the paper's masthead, while Lady Capulet looks like the widow Victoria was to become. The influence of the older Victoria is again evident in the advertisement for *Cassell's Illustrated Shakespeare* edition from *Cassell's Illustrated Almanack*, 1876. Lady Capulet is presented as the aging Queen in a scene of family strife, where Juliet postures as a Victorian heroine in distress.

✳ *The Illustrated Sporting and Dramatic News* for July 27, 1878, offered its patrons a picture supplement that could be detached and framed. It shows a very youthful Juliet pondering the implications of her marriage as she plays with her new wedding ring. The rope ladder that brought Romeo to her room may be seen on the balcony to the lower right. Considering the implications of one's actions is rooted in the Victorian sense of morality.

✳ Nineteenth-century porcelain figurine of Charlotte and Susan Cushman playing Romeo and Juliet. The American sisters premiered in this double role at the Haymarket Theatre, London, in 1846. Their success is indicated on the accompanying playbill advertising their twenty-first performance in these roles on February 17, 1846. Not all remarks were complimentary, however. A reviewer in *Lloyd's Weekly Newspaper* (Feb. 4, 1855) satirizes: "Miss Romeo,—or rather,— Miss Cushman as Romeo, has appeared this week at the Haymarket. The curiosity is not a novelty . . . We could as soon warm our hands at a painted fire, as feel the impetuous passion of an ungowned Romeo," and he concludes by suggesting, "Why should not Mr. Charles Kean play Juliet?"

✳ White silk velvet and iridescent scale dress. Worn by Julia Marlowe as Juliet. Marlowe debuted as Juliet in New York in December, 1887. Her biographer, Charles Edward Russell, wrote: "The effect upon the general audience that night was of a greatly notable achievement, a marvelously beautiful creation, a *Juliet* of a new and commanding eminence."

Mistresses Page and Ford, Anne Page

✳

THE MERRY WIVES OF WINDSOR 1597

Tradition holds that Shakespeare wrote this jolly play at the request of Queen Elizabeth who had delighted in the character of Falstaff in the earlier Henry IV plays. Mistress Ford and Mistress Page are the "merry wives" who play a practical joke on the fat old knight who tries to woo both of them at once. First they hide him in a clothes-basket and have him dumped in the mud; then they disguise him as an old woman. Nineteenth-century opinion found the play a bit "coarse" but judged the two women as "social, merry-hearted, fond of broad jests, but none the less chaste." The romantic interest, young Anne Page, is pretty and modest, but "love teaches even her shyness to be bold" as, like Juliet, she outwits her parents to catch the man she loves, this time with a happy ending.

Detail from Heinrich Lossow (1843–1897), The Merry Wives of Windsor, *Act III, scene iii (1888), English photogravure by Gebbie & Husson Co. of a painting by this German artist.*

✳ Heinrich Lossow (1843–1897), *The Merry Wives of Windsor, Act III, scene iii* (1888), English photogravure by Gebbie & Husson Co. of a painting by this German artist known for his genre scenes. The details of a substantial middle-class German interior relate this work to seventeenth-century Dutch genre paintings, suggesting the earthy and festive qualities of Jan Steen that are so appropriate for this play. Its adoption for an English audience reflects the close relations between the two countries fostered by Victoria's marriage to Prince Albert of Saxe-Coburg-Gotha, and the popularity of German philosophy and Shakespeare studies.

✳ The Reverend Matthew William Peters (1742–1814), Watercolor of Mrs. Page with a letter (Act II, scene i); nineteenth century, after a painting by Peters for the Boydell Gallery (1789).

✳ The Reverend J. R. Pitman, ed., *The School-Shakspeare* (London: C. Rice, 1822). Pitman writes: "The attention of young females . . . has of late years been carefully directed to the study of our English Classics." Accordingly, he presents versions of the plays from which "immoral language has been carefully excluded." For *The Merry Wives of Windsor*, he excerpts scenes that could be read or performed at home or in school. The book is dedicated to Sarah Siddons, whom Pitman greatly admired.

✳ The Reverend Matthew William Peters (1742–1814), Watercolor of Mrs. Ford (Act III, scene iii); nineteenth century, after a painting by Peters for the Boydell Gallery (1791).

✳ Robert Smirke (1752–1845), *The Merry Wives of Windsor*, *Act V, scene v,* engraved by W. Sharpe for the Boydell Shakespeare Gallery (London, 1793). Smirke contributed thirty-two paintings to the Shakespeare Gallery in London that was sponsored by John and Josiah Boydell and opened in 1789. The Boydell paintings were reproduced in sets of engravings, sold separately or used as illustrations to editions of Shakespeare through the next century. Known especially for his depiction of comic scenes, Smirke has here caught the glee of Mistresses Ford and Page as they watch Falstaff's bewildered shock caused by their last joke on the fat knight.

✳ Alfred Concanen (1835–1886), *The Merry Wives of Windsor*. Concanen was a Victorian illustrator who specialized in covers for sheet music, though he also contributed to *The Illustrated Sporting and Dramatic News*. There is a comic cartoon quality about his depiction of a jovial Falstaff making love to both ladies at once, while jealous Master Ford hovers at the door. Mistress Page, pouring his cup of sack, is already plotting the joke at Herne's Oak as she looks at the picture of Herne the Hunter on the wall, while Mistress Ford, who is in on the plot, suffers the knight to take her hand with an expression of humorous wit on her face.

✳ Thomas Francis Dicksee (1819–1895), *Anne Page* (1862), oil painting. Dicksee here chooses the moment in Act I, scene i, when Anne follows her father's request, "Nay, daughter, carry the wine in, we'll drink within." Though her dress is Elizabethan in style, Anne's face has the bright eyes, pink cheeks, and rosebud mouth of a Victorian beauty, and the moment shows her as the ideal daughter, obedient to her father's command.

Portia and Jessica

*

THE MERCHANT OF VENICE 1596–97

Portia and Jessica are two young women who outwit the masculine world of mercantile Venice. Portia follows the wishes of her deceased wealthy father in using the casket test to choose her husband, then disguises herself as a lawyer to turn the tables on Jessica's father, Shylock, the moneylender. Jessica, meanwhile, elopes with the young man of her choice, escaping from the grasp of her father who keeps her locked up at home with his money. Portia was a favorite character for nineteenth-century actresses. Helena Faucit Martin writes in 1880, "Her character combines all the graces of the richest womanhood with the strength of purpose, the wise helpfulness, and sustained power of the noblest manhood . . . it is the woman's keener wit and insight which see into and overcome the difficulty which has perplexed the wisest heads in Venice."

* Artist Unknown, *Shylock and Jessica* (1878). This illustration from an unknown painting, probably reproduced in *The Illustrated Sporting and Dramatic News*, shows an unusual tender moment between Shylock and his daughter. He gives the key to his house and wealth to Jessica for safekeeping while he is away from home, not guessing that she will take the opportunity of his absence to elope with her Christian lover. She looks away from him and out at us, keeping her disobedient thoughts to herself. The artist has captured these Shakespearean characters with beautiful middle-European Jewish features.

* John Dawson Watson (1832–1892), *Portia and Shylock,* Merchant of Venice*, Act IV, scene i*, engraved by C. W. Sharp (London: Cassell & Company, n.d.). Watson was a watercolorist and prolific illustrator. The engraving shown here could have been purchased for individual framing or used for an illustrated edition of Shakespeare. Watson's pleading Shylock with black beard and large knife has more of the qualities of a nineteenth-century stage Jew than the Shylock in the illustration described above. Portia makes her point emphatically, but her features reproduce the soft oval face and rosebud lips of a Victorian maiden.

✳ Two pictures from *The Illustrated London News* of January 13, 1849, record a production of *The Merchant of Venice* for the Queen at Windsor Castle, on December 28, 1848. This was the first performance in a series at Windsor under the direction of Charles Kean: "All this is dear Albert's own idea," as Victoria wrote in her Journal afterwards. Theatrical productions at Windsor were given during the Christmas season and involved the whole family, as can be seen from the four children seated in front of the Queen. Shylock confronts Portia within the play on the left, and the Queen afterward in the larger "play" watched by the courtiers on the right. Of the thirteen Shakespeare plays performed at Windsor during eleven seasons, only *Merchant* and *Macbeth* were presented twice.

✳ Artist Unknown, *Portia*. In this late nineteenth-century colored lithograph, Portia is represented as the "New Woman," looking like one of the early female students at Oxford or Cambridge where the first women were admitted in the 1870s. The artist goes further by opening Portia's academic gown to reveal her shapely legs clad in breeches.

✳ Richard Westall (1765–1836), *Merchant of Venice, Act III, scene ii*, engraved by George Noble for the Boydell Shakespeare Gallery (London, 1796). Westall was a prominent book illustrator and contributed twenty-two paintings to the Boydell Gallery. His interpretation of this scene where Bassanio chooses the correct

casket is influenced by European history painting, such as that produced in eighteenth-century Venice. He captures Portia, not as the stern lawyer, but as the woman in love.

✳ Friedrich Brockmann (b.1809), *Portia and Nerissa* (1849), oil painting. Portia pensively holds the note from the gold casket in her hand, as though she is thinking about her father's last will, that she marry the suitor who chooses the correct casket. Her lady-in-waiting, Nerissa, holds the correct lead casket while she looks supportively at her mistress. William Pressly has pointed out that Brockmann's painting owes much to the tradition of pairing two idealized women.

✳ Franz-Xaver Barth (1821–1894), *The Casket Scene–Merchant of Venice*, painting reproduced in a supplement to *The Illustrated London News*, March 20, 1875. Barth was a well-known Bavarian who specialized in history painting. The blond Portia highlighted here is again not the lawyer, but the love-sick nineteenth-century maiden, her flowing hair suggesting virginity, her hand to her mouth as she awaits Bassanio's decision with some agitation. Even more than Westall's painting, Barth's work has a feel of the stage-set; we, and the members of Portia's household, watch this play unfold.

Artist Unknown, Portia,
late nineteenth-century colored lithograph.

Katherine

✳

THE TAMING OF THE SHREW 1593–94

Ada Rehan (1860–1916) as Kate in The Taming of the Shrew, *photograph (c.1887)*

Petulant Katherine and mild Bianca are about as unlike as any two sisters can be. While many of Shakespeare's heroines defy their fathers to marry the men of their choice, only Kate is stubborn, loud-mouthed, and disinclined to marry at all. She is dragged kicking and screaming to the altar by Petruchio, and when she gives her final speech about a wife's duty to her husband, we wonder if she is *really* "tamed." Nineteenth-century writers saw in her behavior the lack of a mother's influence on her upbringing. The American, Henrietta Lee Palmer, wrote in 1858: "It is scarcely possible to consider the character of Katharina with gravity; her shrewishness is so wildly extravagant, so inconceivable in any maiden, 'young, beauteous, and brought up as best becomes a gentlewoman,' that she may serve but as the heroine of the extravaganza wherein she figures."

One of the most famous Katherines of all time was the Irish/American actress Ada Rehan (1860–1916), whose career was developed by the New York manager-director, Augustin Daly. The theater critic William Winter wrote, "it was her impersonation of Katherine, in 'The Taming of the Shrew,' that decisively established her rank as a great actress of comedy." The play was first presented at Daly's Theatre on January 18, 1887, and ran for 121 performances. John Drew played Petruchio.

✻ Autograph letter from Ada Rehan to Augustin Daly, April 10, 1887. "I have learned to love my profession through you for I never knew it as an art untill [sic] I met you. Then came ambition." The letter is tipped-in to an edition of *The Taming of the Shrew* published to celebrate its one hundredth performance, "as arranged by Augustin Daly with an Introduction by William Winter" (New York: Privately Printed for Mr. Daly, 1887).

✻ Playbill, Daly's Theatre, *The Taming of the Shrew*, Tuesday, January 18, 1887. This playbill, specially printed on silk, marks the opening night of Ada Rehan's famous run as Katherine.

✻ William Shakespeare, *The Taming of the Shrew*, "Players' Edition," with an Introduction by Ada Rehan (New York: Doubleday, Page & Co., 1900). Rehan's comments on the character she played so often are insightful:
Katharine's own words point out her fine intelligence, which places her far beyond the common acceptation of the word 'Shrew.' I look upon her as a grand creature—a very noble nature—of high breeding—a spoiled, wilful child who had always had her own way with every one. It has been thought that Katharine's submission was too abject, but I have looked upon it that she proportioned her penance to her offences; and that, having been more outrageous in temper than mortal woman was ever known to be, she adopted more humility than woman need ever show.

✻ Photographs from the Daly production showing Rehan in her costume as Kate and the typical elaborate nineteenth-century stage set, just at the moment in Act II, scene i, which reads in Daly's version:
Kath. I chase you, if I tarry; let me go.
[Crosses to go.
Pet. Nay, Kate; in sooth, you 'scape not so.
[Holds her.

From an extra-illustrated edition of William Shakspere, *Taming of the Shrew* (New York: Privately Printed for Mr. Daly, 1887).

Ellen Tree   Friday October 21st 1836

Rosalind and Celia

*

AS YOU LIKE IT 1599

Rosalind, daughter and niece of dukes, disguises herself in boy's attire when she is banished from her uncle's court. Accompanied by her cousin, Celia, and the Fool, Touchstone, she travels in the Forest of Arden where she teaches her lover, Orlando, the art of wooing. There she is also reunited with her banished father, and all ends "as you like it" with a triple wedding. Rosalind has been a favorite "breeches" role for actresses from Peg Woffington in the eighteenth century to Katherine Hepburn in our own. Comparing her with Portia in *Merchant*, Anna Jameson says, "Portia is dignified, splendid and romantic; Rosalind is playful, pastoral and picturesque." By contrast, Celia is "more quiet and retired" but "full of sweetness, kindness, and intelligence."

Richard James Lane (1800–1872), Ellen Tree. Friday October 21st 1836. Rosalind. *Colored lithograph (London: J. Mitchell, Dec.1, 1838).*

* Richard James Lane (1800–1872), *Ellen Tree. Friday October 21st 1836. Rosalind.* Colored lithograph (London: J. Mitchell, Dec.1, 1838). Ellen Tree (1805–1880) seems to have performed Rosalind first during an American tour, 1836–1839. She was used to cross-dressing, as she had earlier played Romeo to Fanny Kemble's Juliet and proved herself adept at fencing. After she married Charles Kean, they embarked on a highly successful theatrical career together and were Queen Victoria's performers of choice.

* *Shakspeare's As You Like It, A Comedy; Revised by J. P. Kemble: And Now Published As It Is Performed At The Theatres Royal* (N.p.: n.d.). Prompt copy belonging to Helen Faucit who signed her name on the front cover. Faucit first played Rosalind at Covent Garden in 1839 when she was twenty-two years old for her benefit performance. The page opening at Act IV, scene iii, indicates the kind of cuts that were used on the nineteenth-century stage; eliminated is Orlando's exchange with Rosalind about kissing. In her later essay on "Rosalind" Faucit writes: "The device [doublet and hose] to which she resorted seemed to

suggest itself irresistibly; and, armed with Shakespeare's words, it was an intense pleasure to try to give expression to the archness, the wit, the quick ready intellect, the ebullient fancy, with the tenderness underlying all, which give to this scene its transcendent charm."

✳ Playbill, Theatre Royal, Drury Lane. *As You Like It*, Friday, April 13, 1787. This playbill advertises a benefit performance for Mrs. Jordan who is appearing here for the first time as Rosalind. It is interesting that both she and later Helen Faucit premiered in this role at their benefits.

✳ Henry William Bunbury (1750–1811), *As You Like It*, engraved by C. Knight (London: W. Dickinson, December 20, 1788). Bunbury dedicated this engraving to Mrs. Jordan, shown to the right dressed in the height of fashion as an "Empire" dandy, "In Gratitude for the Pleasure receiv'd from her Inimitable Performance of Rosalind." Dorothy Jordan (1761–1816) was to comedy what Sarah Siddons was for tragedy—the leading actress of her day. She was a hard worker, always striving to support her extended family, and frequently played during pregnancies, though she was especially well-known for her "breeches" roles.

✳ Handcolored "penny plain" print of *Mrs. H. Johnston as Rosalind in 'As You Like It'* (London: W. West at his Theatrical Print Warehouse, March 20, 1813). Nannette Parker Johnston (b.1782) was an accomplished actress and horsewoman who played a variety of roles, many as a team with her husband, Henry Harris Johnston. At the time of this print, they were engaged by Covent Garden Theatre.

After fifteen years of marriage and six children, she struck out on her own in 1811, went through affairs with three other men (always climbing the social ladder), and eventually retired from the stage around 1816.

✳ William Heath (1795–1840), *Miss Walstein as Rosalind*, handcolored engraving (London: T. Palser, June 18, 1815). Eliza Walstein (d.1833) was a popular comic star on the Dublin stage in the early nineteenth century.

✳ Bilston enamel circular medallion, mounted on turned wood box (c.1790). *En grisaille*, depicting Mrs. Dorothy Jordan wearing high-crowned hat and riding coat. Gift of Mrs. Robin Craven.

Beatrice

✳

MUCH ADO ABOUT NOTHING 1598–99

"Beatrice is one of the most charming creations of Shakspeare's wit," writes M. Leigh Noel. "She is a woman of great activity [and] high animal spirits." Like Rosalind, she lives with her cousin, Hero, in the home of her uncle. Here she meets the worldly and witty Benedick, back from the wars, but she is a match for him and for the weaker Claudio who deserts Hero at the altar. Both men get their women in the end, but not without some teasing of Beatrice and Benedick. Anna Jameson, while noting "a touch of insolence" in her wit, says that Beatrice's "biting jests" amuse us the more because she "who thought a man of God's making not good enough for her," stoops "like the rest of her sex, taming her wild heart to the loving hand of him whom she had scorned."

✳ Artist Unknown, Watercolor of *Ellen Terry as Beatrice* (n.d.). Terry felt that she played Beatrice much better before she joined forces with Henry Irving at the Lyceum Theatre in London. "He gave me little help. Beatrice must be swift, swift, swift! Owing to Henry's rather finicking, deliberate method as Benedick, I could never put the right pace into my part."

✳ Hal Ludlow, *'Much Ado About Nothing' at the Lyceum*, illustration for *The Pictorial World*, October 21, 1882. The scene depicts Ellen Terry as Beatrice announcing to Henry Irving as Benedick, "Against my will I am sent to bid you come in to dinner." See the prompt book for this production below.

✳ Sir John Gilbert (1817–1897), *'Sigh No More Ladies,'* Much ado about Nothing, *Act II, scene iii*, colored lithograph of drawing (London, Edinburgh & Glasgow: William Mackenzie, n.d.). Gilbert's skills as an accomplished illustrator are evident here as he creates a scene out of a song in the play. "Sigh no more, ladies, sigh no more,/ Men were deceivers ever," inspired this picture of an angry young woman overhearing the man who was evidently her lover wooing another lady.

Thomas Stothard (1755–1834), attributed,
Beatrice Listening in the Arbour, Much Ado About Nothing,
Act III, scene i (c.1820–1830), pen-and-ink drawing.

✳ William Shakespeare, *Much Ado About Nothing . . . arranged for the stage by Henry Irving, and Presented at the Lyceum Theatre, On Wednesday, October 11th, 1882* (London: The Chiswick Press, 1882). Prompt copy belonging to Sir Henry Irving with his signature on the flyleaf. The book is open to the famous bantering scene (Act IV, scene i) between Beatrice and Benedick. Irving has included instructions for kissing, seizing, or taking Beatrice's hand in several places throughout the scene.

✳ Thomas Stothard (1755–1834), attributed, *Beatrice Listening in the Arbour,* Much Ado About Nothing, *Act III, scene i* (c.1820–1830), pen-and-ink drawing. This drawing comes from an album of original drawings illustrating Shakespeare's plays by Thomas Stothard and others, who are not identified. Stothard did a number of illustrations for the plays, and this one shows him working out the dynamics of a female figure crouched in hiding.

✳ Helena Faucit Martin, *On Beatrice* (Printed for Strictly Private Circulation, 1885). Martin originally wrote this essay as a letter to John Ruskin. She says that Beatrice's "character is not to me so engaging," as that of Rosalind. Beatrice "has not learned tenderness or toleration." "She has a quick eye to see what is weak or ludicrous in man or woman. The impulse to speak out the smart and poignant things that rise readily and swiftly to her lips, is irresistible. She does not mean to inflict pain . . . She simply rejoices in the keen sword-play of her wit, as she would in any other exercise of her intellect or sport of her fancy."

Olivia and Viola

✳

TWELFTH NIGHT 1601–02

This play shows us the processes by which two women work through their grief over the deaths of their brothers: the Countess Olivia for a brother who has actually died, and Viola for a twin brother whom she fears may have perished in the same storm that threw her on the coast of Illyria. Olivia hides behind the veils of mourning and refuses to hear the entreaties of Duke Orsino for her hand, while Viola dresses as the boy Sebastian and offers her service to the Duke in order to make her way in the world. When she comes to court Olivia on behalf of Orsino, Olivia falls in love with Viola/Sebastian, while Viola has fallen in love with Orsino. The gender-bending plot rights itself with the eventual appearance of Viola's lost twin brother who happily marries Olivia, leaving the Duke for Viola. The waiting-gentle-woman Maria adds humor and warmth to the play through her witty dealings with Malvolio and Sir Toby Belch, Olivia's kinsman.

White, Julia Marlowe as Viola in Twelfth Night *(n.d.), photograph. Julia Marlowe (1866–1950) first played Viola in 1887.*

✳ Artist Unknown, *Twelfth Night, Act III, scene i.* (n.d., c.1850), colored engraving. The artist here shows one of the most intimate moments between Viola and Olivia. Viola, dressed as the young courtier, Sebastian, has come to woo Olivia on behalf of her master, Orsino, but Olivia falls in love with the disguised Viola instead, and reaches her hand towards his pouch to give him some money.

✳ Artist Unknown, *Twelfth Night, Act III, scene iv* (n.d., c.1880), colored lithograph. The artist captures the pleasure on the faces of Olivia and her gentlewoman, Maria, as they wait to see Malvolio in his yellow stockings with crossed garters.

✳ Kenny Meadows (1790–1874), *Viola,* (original c.1836), colored engraving.

✳ Kenny Meadows (1790–1874), *Olivia,* (original c.1836), colored engraving.

These two engravings were part of the original "beauties" sets depicting Shakespeare's heroines, published in 1836–37 by Charles Heath. They were reproduced widely throughout the nineteenth century and are here presented as finely-colored individual engravings meant for framing and hanging in the home.

✻ White, *Julia Marlowe as Viola in* Twelfth Night, (n.d.), photograph. Julia Marlowe (1866–1950) was born Sarah Frances Frost in England, moved to America as a child, and first played Viola in 1887. A contemporary male critic noted, "Her vivacity and humor carried her successfully through the comic adventures, but the essential feminine charm of it frequently eluded her." Did she show too much of the "New Woman" in her interpretation of this cross-dressed role? Another (male) critic, however, wrote that her Viola was "one of the most nearly perfect impersonations in her Shakespearean repertory . . . ."

✻ William Shakespeare, *Twelfth Night* (N.p.: n.d., c.1887). Prompt copy from a production with E. H. Sothern and Julia Marlowe. The book is open at Act I, scene v, Viola's first conference with Olivia where Olivia lifts her veil. Viola's line "What I am, and what I would, [are as secret as maidenhead]" has had the bracketed part cut to remove what was considered coarse and offensive language at the time.

✻ Charles Robert Leslie (1794–1859), *Olivia* (n.d.), painting, engraved by T. Vernon. Leslie was an accomplished artist and member of the Royal Academy who also painted for Queen Victoria. Olivia lifting her veil at Sebastian/Viola's request became a major iconographic image for *Twelfth Night*. Leslie depicts Olivia in the "beauties" tradition, looking every bit the young Victorian widow.

✻ Crimson velvet brocade coat and vest; red satin trousers; silk scarf. Worn by Ada Rehan as Viola in *Twelfth Night*. Augustin Daly's production of this play premiered in New York in 1893, where it ran for six weeks, then moved to London for another 100 performances. Reviews of Rehan as Viola, however, were mixed. Charles Shattuck writes, "There was no room in Viola for the explosiveness of her Katherine nor for the wit and merriment of her Rosalind. Viola, confined to a dramatic situation which she cannot dominate, has to be rescued from it; and Miss Rehan, thus prevented from lifting and carrying the play, was subdued by it."

Ophelia

✳

HAMLET 1600–01

Ophelia is one of the saddest heroines of Shakespeare's plays. With the departure of her brother Laertes to France, she is left without a friend or confidant to face the erratic and violent behavior of her lover, Hamlet, and the untimely death of her foolish old father, Polonius. Hamlet's mother, Gertrude, caught up in the tangle of her own feelings for her second husband Claudius, cannot serve as a mother-figure for the lonely young woman. Overcome by grief and confusion, Ophelia's mind breaks, and she falls to her watery death while trying to hang a flower garland over the stream. This view of Ophelia as the innocent victim is typical of the nineteenth century. Anna Jameson writes of her: "O far too soft, too good, too fair, to be cast among the briers of this working-day world, and fall and bleed upon the thorns of life!"

✳ Henry Tresham (1751–1814), *Ophelia vide Hamlet*, etching by F. Bartolozzi, colored (London: M. Bovi, August 1, 1794). Tresham's illustration of Act IV, scene vii, of the play places Ophelia within a classical or French romantic tradition. The madness that inspired her bawdy songs has, in Tresham's view, also made her disheveled and wanton in appearance. At the same time, the wreath of flowers and her eyes raised to heaven suggest the divine inspiration of a poetic muse.

✳ J. Gear (fl.1800), *Ophelia Before her Suicide*, original pen-and-ink sketch. Like Tresham's more finished etching, Gear's sketch shows Ophelia moments before she drowns in the stream, but Gear's Ophelia seems less divinely inspired and more distraught. The vegetation closes in menacingly around her as she attempts to hang onto the willow limbs. The artist of this book of sketches of Shakespearean scenes may be the J. C. Gear whose *Shakespeare's Beautiful Idea on the Seven Ages of Man* was published in 1792. The Folger volume of sketches is dated c.1814.

H.Tresham A.Inv.

OPHELIA Vide HAMLET

There on the pendant boughs her coronet weeds
Clambering to hang an envious sliver broke;

When down her weedy trophies
Fell in the weeping brook

London Published Aug.t 1 1794, by M.r Bovi, N.o 97 Pecadille near S.t Pauls Church.

Etch'd by F. Bartolozzi A.

* Liverpool Delft transfer-printed tile, *Mrs. Lessingham in the character of Ophelia* (c.1777–1780). Gift of Mrs. Robin Craven. These sets of tiles printed with pictures of actors and actresses in well-known roles seem to have been popular during the eighteenth century. Jane Hemet Lessingham (1739?–1783) played a number of roles, primarily at Covent Garden Theatre. Outside the theater she was reported to have frequented coffee houses dressed in men's clothing. This picture of her as Ophelia is based on a drawing from life by James Roberts (1753–c.1809) that was engraved by C. Grignion for Bell's edition of Shakespeare, 1775.

* Jacques Jean Marie Achille Deveria (1800–1857) and Louis Boulanger (1807–1867), *Hamlet, Acte IV, scène v* (c.1827), colored lithograph by Henri Gaugain. One of ten illustrations from Shakespeare that appeared in F. L. Moreau, *Souvenirs du Théâtre Anglais à Paris* (Paris: Henri Gaugain, Lambert et al, 1827). The book was prepared as a souvenir honoring the visit of an English company of actors to Paris. Charles Kemble and Harriet Smithson starred as Hamlet and Ophelia. The French, who were used to Charles Ducis's watered-down version of Shakespeare, reacted with shocked surprise to the tremendous emotion with which Smithson presented Ophelia's madness: "there was utter silence among the profoundly moved spectators."

Henry Tresham (1751–1814), Ophelia vide Hamlet, *etching by F. Bartolozzi, colored (London: M. Bovi, August 1, 1794).*

Liverpool Delft transfer-printed tile,
Mrs. Lessingham in the character of Ophelia *(c.1777–1780).*
Gift of Mrs. Robin Craven.

* John Hayter (1800–1891), *Ophelia*, drawing, engraved by W. H. Mote originally for the second set of Heath's "beauties" from Shakespeare (1848). This picture was used to illustrate the New York 1850 edition of Anna Jameson's *Characteristics of Women*. She is depicted as a fragile young woman, more withdrawn and melancholy than outwardly violent in her madness.

* D. Crentacoste, *Ophelia* (c.1898), engraved by S. Dreher. To twentieth-century eyes, a death-mask of a character who never even lived seems bizarre or macabre, but death-masks were a popular genre in the nineteenth century, and representations of dead women became a topos in the art of the period. Elizabeth Bronfen writes that the fascination with such representations of the female body "has to do with the fact that the two enigmas of western culture, death and female sexuality, are here 'contained' in a [non-threatening] way . . . ." In Ophelia's case, she can be seen as pure and virginal in her death sleep—and thus more comfortably the nineteenth-century female ideal—as opposed to frightening and violent in her madness.

* Monogrammist T. E., *Ophelia* (n.d.), oil painting. In his *Catalogue of Paintings in the Folger Shakespeare Library*, William Pressly suggests that the painting dates from about 1880, and that the style indicates the artist was Continental. We see Ophelia face-on, and rather than a beauty, it is the face of a sad, distracted young woman bent on making her way to her watery death. Richard Altick has noted that Ophelia was the most popular of Shakespeare's heroines for nineteenth-century painters. Later in the century, when photography became the vogue, young women in insane asylums were posed as Ophelia in photographic portraits.

Lady Macbeth

✳

MACBETH 1606

Lady Macbeth, with her aggressiveness and murderous instincts turned to madness, was one of the most difficult of Shakespeare's heroines for the nineteenth century to appropriate. Generally the century either distanced her by placing her within the context of the barbarous Middle Ages, or they redeemed her as a woman who wanted too much for her husband, was discarded by him after his success, and died lonely and mad. M. Leigh Noel writes in her fine study of Lady Macbeth: "she remained a woman singled out by destiny to become an example of the torture of unconfessed sin and the bitterness of unlawful ambition . . . Does not one feel intense commiseration for the criminal? . . . She had loved, had sinned, had suffered, and now she dies in complete desolation and despair."

Detail from Valentine Walter Bromley (1848–1877), Macbeth and Lady Macbeth, engraved by G. Goldberg (London: Cassell & Co., n.d.).

One of the greatest interpreters of Lady Macbeth in the history of English theater was the actress Sarah Siddons (1755–1831). She first performed the role in February 1785 at Drury Lane at the age of thirty, when she was about five months pregnant. Her original notes on the character unfortunately are lost, but she gave them to her first biographer, Thomas Campbell, and we do have contemporary or near-contemporary accounts of her peformance. In the Folger Library is a copy of *Macbeth* interleaved with notes by a professor of law, George Joseph Bell, who saw her perform in Edinburgh. Anna Jameson writes: "Mrs. Siddons left among her papers [an] analysis of the character of Lady Macbeth, which I have never seen; but I have heard her say, that after playing the part for thirty years, she never read it over without discovering in it something new . . . ." Various commentators note the discrepancy between Siddons' own view of Lady Macbeth and her actual performance on stage. Siddons conceived of the character as fair-haired and with "all the charms and graces of personal beauty . . . feminine, nay, even fragile," but the effect she had on her audiences was quite different. Hazlitt recalled, "Vice was never so solitary and so grand. The step, look, voice of the Royal

Theatre Royal, Drury Lane.

This present TUESDAY, April 22, 1794,
His Majesty's Servants will perform *Shakspeare's*

MACBETH.

With the Original Music of MATTHEW LOCK,
and Accompaniments by Dr. ARNE and Mr. LINLEY.
Duncan, *King of Scotland.* Mr. BENSLEY,
Malcolm, Mr. C. KEMBLE, Donalbain, Master DE CAMP,
Macbeth by Mr. KEMBLE.
Banquo by Mr. WROUGHTON,
Macduff by Mr. PALMER,
Lenox, Mr. WHITFIELD. Rosse, Mr. BARRYMORE,
Fleance, Master GREGSON, Siward, Mr. AICKIN,
Seyton, Mr. BENSON, Physician, Mr. PACKER,
Officer, Mr. BANKS, Serjeant, Mr. CAULFIELD,
First Murderer, Mr. Phillimore, Second Murderer, Mr Webb,
Lady Macbeth by Mrs. SIDDONS,
Gentlewoman by Miss TIDSWELL.
Hecate by Mr. BANNISTER,
1Witch, Mr MOODY, 2 Witch, Mr DODD, 3 Witch Mr SUETT
CHORUS of WITCHES and SPIRITS,
Mrs. Crouch, Mrs. Bland, Miss Leak, Miss Arne, Miss Menage,
Miss Granger, Miss Chatterley, Miss Redhead, Miss Gawdry, Mrs. Bramwell,
Mrs. Butler, &c. &c.
Mr. Kelly, Master Welsh, Mr. Sedgwick, Mr. Dignum, Mr. Cooke, Mr. Biggs,
Mr. Trueman, Mr. Evans, Mr. Lyons, Mr. Maddocks, Mr. Welsh, Mr. Danby.
The SCENERY, MACHINERY, and HABITS are entirely New.
Painters, Messrs. GREENWOOD, MALTON, CATTON, CAPON,
BUZARGLO, FRENCH, EDWARDS, and their Assistants.
Machinist, Mr. CARBONEL.
The Dresses and Decorations are Executed by Mr. JOHNSTON.
An Occasional Prologue and Epilogue,
To be Spoken by Mr. KEMBLE, and Miss FARREN,
After the Tragedy, will be performed a FARCE, called

The VIRGIN UNMASK'D.

Goodwill by Mr. Packer, Blister Mr. Suett,
Coupee by Mr. Bannister, Jun. Quaver by Mr. Dignum,
Thomas by Mr. Benson. Miss Lucy by Mrs. Bland.
Boxes 6s, Second Price 3s—Pit 3s 6d Second Price 2s—Gal 2s Second Price 1s.
Upper Gal. 1s. Second Price 6d.
No MONEY to be RETURNED.
✱ A New and accurate Edition of the Play, to be had at the Theatre.
Places for the Boxes to be taken of Mr FOSBROOK, Little Russel-Street,
The Doors to be opened at a Quarter past Five, and to begin at a Quarter past Six.
Vivant Rex et Regina!

Playbill, Theatre Royal, Drury Lane, Macbeth,
*Tuesday, April 22, 1794. Sarah Siddons as Lady Macbeth
and Charles Kemble as Macbeth.*

Murderess forces our eye after them as if of a being from a darker world, full of evil, but full of power—unconnected with life, but come to do its deed of darkness, and then pass away." Hazlitt's comments suggest that the effect of Siddons' almost supernatural power owes something to the Witches in the play.

✳ Anonymous, *Sarah Siddons as Lady Macbeth* (c.1790–1810), oil painting. This painting, based on Act II, scene ii of the play, shows Lady Macbeth taking the dagger from her fearful husband so that she can return to the murder site and place it by the sleeping groom. William Pressly suggests that this "commanding woman of statuesque bearing and penetrating stare" is very likely based on the character as played by Sarah Siddons.

✳ George Henry Harlow (1787–1819), *Mrs. Siddons*, engraved by Robert Cooper (London: H. Berthoud, Sept. 28, 1822). This picture shows her in the famous "sleepwalking scene," Act V, scene i. Siddons said of Lady Macbeth at this moment: "Her ever-restless spirit wanders in troubled dreams about her dismal apartment; and whether waking or asleep, the smell of innocent blood incessantly haunts her imagination."

✳ Playbill, Theatre Royal, Drury Lane, *Macbeth,* Tuesday, April 22, 1794. Sarah Siddons and Charles Kemble play the leads in this production, which includes a Chorus of more than twenty witches, half of them female, while the three main Witches are played by male actors. The staging of *Macbeth* as a kind of tragic musical was not uncommon in the eighteenth century.

✳ George Joseph Bell (1770–1843), annotated copy of William Shakspeare, *Macbeth . . . with remarks by Mrs. Inchbald* (London: for Longman, Hurst, et al, c.1806). Bell's comments on Act II, scene i, when Macbeth reports on his murder of Duncan, show his detailed observation. "Mrs. Siddons here displays her wonderfull power & knowledge of nature. As if her inhuman strength of spirit [were] overcome by the contagion of his remorse and terror. Her arms about her neck & bosom, shuddering."

✳ Kenny Meadows (1790–1874), *Lady Macbeth*, engraving by W. H. Mote, colored. Meadows' original drawing was made for Charles Heath's second set of Shakespeare heroine "beauties" in 1848. Though scowling and holding a bloody dagger, this Lady Macbeth with her soft face of finely-chiseled features and her delicate hand evokes the cult of physical frailty which, by mid-century, "was a sign of respectable femininity." This is the Lady Macbeth of Edward Dowden, the critic, who writes of "her delicate frame . . . filled with high-strung nervous energy," and "her little hand" from which she tries to remove the stain of blood at which "her delicate sense sicken[s]" (1875).

✳ Valentine Walter Bromley (1848–1877), *Macbeth and Lady Macbeth*, engraved by G. Goldberg (London: Cassell & Co., n.d.). Bromley's painting combines two nineteenth-century views of Lady Macbeth. The costumes, furniture and wall painting set her within the barbaric medieval past, but her expression of loyalty and comfort towards Macbeth conveys the Victorian view espoused by M. Leigh Noel when writing about Lady Macbeth, that her ambition was all for her husband.

Richard J. Lane (1800–1872),
Jane Shirreff, Priscilla Horton and Harriett Taylor as Singing Witches,
drawing, first published London: J. Mitchell, December 1, 1838.
Based on a production of Macbeth *staged at Covent Garden*
during the 1837–38 season.

❋ Henry Fuseli (1741–1825), *The Weird Sisters* (1783), painting; gravure (London: Gebbie & Husson Co., 1887). Fuseli's painting was reproduced a number of times, well into the nineteenth century. He shows the Witches, "each at once her choppy finger/ laying upon her skinny lips," but his figures look more male than female, representing old crones at an androgynous age. His picture suggests how the Witches could have been depicted on stage by actors, as in the productions with Sarah Siddons and later.

❋ Richard J. Lane (1800–1872), Jane Shirreff, Priscilla Horton and Harriett D. Taylor as *Singing Witches*, colored lithograph (first published London: J. Mitchell, December 1, 1838). These three attractive young women appeared in the Chorus of Witches that, in typical nineteenth-century style, was part of Macready's production of *Macbeth* at the Theatre Royal, Covent Garden, during the 1837–38 season. They provide a stark contrast to Fuseli's masculine Witches and suggest another line of representation that leads to the sexually seductive Witches of some twentieth-century productions.

❋ Richard Westall (1766–1836), *Lady Macbeth With a Letter*, oil painting, engraved by James Parker (London: J. & J. Boydell, June 4, 1800). Westall's painting was displayed in the Boydell Shakespeare Gallery and reproduced hundreds of times in large and small engravings. It is based on Sarah Siddons' depiction of Lady Macbeth in Act I, scene v: "Come to my woman's breasts,/ And take my milk for gall, you murd'ring ministers."

A New and Superior Large Paper, Large Type Edition of

CASSELL'S ILLUSTRATED SHAKESPEARE,

Edited, with Notes, by Mr. and Mrs. COWDEN CLARKE, and containing about 500 *Illustrations by* H. C. SELOUS, *will be published in Monthly Parts, price* 7d., *and in Weekly Numbers, price* 1½d.

OTHELLO AND DESDEMONA.   (See *Cassell's Illustrated Shakespeare.*)

*** A LARGE PRESENTATION PLATE, *consisting of a* SHAKESPEARIAN REPRESENTATION *before* QUEEN ELIZABETH, *will be issued,* FREE OF CHARGE, *with* PART I., *and purchasers of* Nos. 1 to 4 *will also be entitled to receive the Plate.*

CASSELL, PETTER, & GALPIN, LONDON, PARIS, AND NEW YORK.

Desdemona

✳

OTHELLO 1604

Desdemona, sheltered daughter of Brabantio, a Venetian senator, is swept off her feet by the exotic tales of the handsome Moorish soldier, Othello. The two marry, and on her pleading, he takes her to his post in Cyprus. Their golden honeymoon is spoiled, however, by the evil insinuations of Othello's lieutenant, Iago, that Desdemona has been unfaithful to her husband. Torn by doubt and jealousy, Othello murders his wife, only to repent after he has "put out the light." M. Leigh Noel sees Desdemona as having "a quick and ready wit, much decision of character, romantic devotion to the man of her choice, . . . and a mind trained to habits of housewifely industry," while Anna Jameson describes her as a woman without "the slightest manifestation of intellectual power . . . a victim consecrated from the first . . . all harmony, all grace, all purity, all tenderness, all truth!"

Advertisement from The Publishers' Circular, *December 8, 1873, for* Cassell's Illustrated Shakespeare, *showing a scene from* Othello.

✳ Henry Liverseege (1803–1832), *Othello & Desdemona*, painting, engraved by J. E. Coombs (Manchester, n.d.). Desdemona is here depicted as a young Victoria trying to charm Othello while Iago lurks in the background. Othello's physical appearance and dress reflect the influence of Orientalism on nineteenth-century Europe. The inscription from the publisher dedicates the engraving to Joseph Marsland, Esq., who owned the original painting. Marsland was most likely one of the *nouveau-riche* Manchester industrialists who collected art for his home.

✳ Advertisement from *The Publishers' Circular*, December 8, 1873, for *Cassell's Illustrated Shakespeare*. Desdemona is represented here as the clinging, loving Victorian wife. Both she and the court woman to her left, who is probably Nerissa, have the graceful necks and facial features of nineteenth-century beauties.

✳ Charles West Cope (1811–1890), *Othello Relating His Adventures*, painting, engraved by T. Vernon (London: Vertue & Co., c.1854). Cope exhibited this painting at the Royal Academy in 1853. It is similar in style and iconography to a painting

Political Cartoon, The New Othello, *in* Pat, *March 26, 1881.*
The cartoon relates to Prime Minister Gladstone's
Land Act of 1881 to help Irish tenants and landowners.

by Henry Fradelle on the same subject, exhibited at the Royal Academy in 1824. Desdemona here is still the respectful young daughter seated next to her father, but her fascination with Othello's tales is revealed in the incline of her head and focus of her eyes on this strange man.

* Staffordshire figurine, *Othello Relating His Adventures*, (c.1850–1860). This decorative figurine replicates the iconography of paintings by Cope and others, and indicates the great popularity of Othello's description of his wooing in Act I, scene iii: "She'd come again, and with a greedy ear/ Devour up my discourse."

* Alexandre Cabanel (1823–1889), *Desdemona*, lithograph (1881) by George Barrie. Cabanel was a French painter known for his fashionable portraits, especially of the members of the court of Napoleon III. His *Desdemona* could be any nineteenth-century beauty depicted with clasped hands and tear-stained face in the guise of a suffering saint. A French writer of the time described Desdemona as "the woman become lover and wife, almost the same day, a charming type of the young *femme anglaise*, ardent without brilliance, tender and devoted without any particular demonstration." To this description Anna Jameson would add, "All that can render misery heart-breaking is assembled round Desdemona."

* Political Cartoon, *The New Othello*, in *Pat*, March 26, 1881. Prime Minister Gladstone as Othello comes to coerce Desdemona as Irish Liberty. A number of political cartoons during the Victorian period draw on Shakespeare's characters to make their point. In this instance, Gladstone, who sympathized with the Irish, is trying to keep them from violent uprising while he prepares his Land League bill that will lead to the Land Act of 1881, which in effect set up dual ownership of land between tenants and landlords in Ireland.

* James Clarke Hook (1819–1907), *Othello's Description of Desdemona* (c.1852), oil painting. A member of the Royal Academy, Hook specialized in literary and marine scenes. William Pressly has pointed out that he was drawn to Shakespeare's Venetian plays, and a contemporary critic commented, "Mr. Hook . . . seems so enamoured of Venetian colouring that his only book might be Othello or Portia." Pressly also notes that the painting draws on the popular iconography of the Garden of Love. Here we have Othello and Desdemona together in their first hours of love, without the intrusive company of her father.

Cleopatra

✳

ANTONY AND CLEOPATRA 1606–07

Cleopatra, Queen of Egypt, who seduces the warrior Antony away from his Roman world, has long been a character who fascinates through her "infinite variety." The nineteenth century had to deal with her blatant sensuality in an age that valued women's modesty. Anna Jameson praised her "mental accomplishments, . . . her woman's wit and woman's wiles . . . her magnificent spirit . . . the gorgeous eastern coloring of the character," but she also warned, "we are conscious of a kind of fascination against which our moral sense rebels, but from which there is no escape." George Sand, the French woman noted for her own freedom of expression, both sexually and socially, understood Cleopatra perfectly: "In the moral order, she represents pure passion; in the historic order, pure tyranny," and she admired this mixture.

Detail from Sarah Bernhardt (1844–1923) as Cleopatra, photograph (N.p., n.d.). Bernhardt played Cleopatra in Shakespeare's Antony and Cleopatra *and in Sardou's extravaganza,* Cléopatre.

✳ Kenny Meadows (1790–1874), *Cleopatra,* engraving by J. Brown, colored (original c.1848). This picture is from the second "beauties" set by Charles Heath, first published in 1848. It appeared as an illustration to Anna Jameson's *Characteristics of Women* in the New York, 1850 edition. Here we see Cleopatra as an Oriental beauty, looking seductively over her bare shoulder, very much in the style of the exotic beauties drawn to illustrate Byron's poems.

✳ Sarah Bernhardt (1844–1923) as Cleopatra, photograph (N.p.; n.d.). The famous French actress played Cleopatra both in Shakespeare's play and in an extravaganza of costume and scenery created for her by Victorien Sardou in 1890, which she performed in Paris and London. Gold and Fizdale, in their recent biography, recount an incident from the London production: "After watching Sarah as Cleopatra, lasciviously entwined in her lover's arms, an elderly dowager was heard to say: 'How unlike, how *very* unlike the home life of our own dear queen!'"

Ann Seymour Damer (1748–1828), Antony & Cleopatra,
Act V, scene ii, *bas relief, engraved by Thomas Hellyer*
(London: J. & J. Boydell, June 4, 1803).

✳ Gold belt in the form of a snake. Worn by the polish actress, Helena Modjeska (1840–1909) when she played Cleopatra. Modjeska premiered in her own production of *Antony and Cleopatra* in San Francisco in September 1898. A local newspaper reviewer wrote: *"Madame Modjeska's Cleopatra is unique. It is purely modern in conception and execution: it is far away from the generally heavy and haughty queen we have seen in the few cases where the play has been presented in the last quarter of a century . . . Madame Modjeska takes, of course, the cue of Cleopatra's sensual nature, but surely never an artist achieved the representation of that more certainly with such exquisite taste and delicacy."*

✳ Ann Seymour Damer (1748–1828), *Antony & Cleopatra, Act V, scene ii,* bas relief, engraved by Thomas Hellyer (London: J. & J. Boydell, June 4, 1803). Ann Damer was one of three women artists associated with the Boydell Shakespeare Gallery, for which she designed two sculpture bas reliefs that were used on the building in which the Gallery was housed and also as designs for the title pages of the sets of engravings. Her depiction of the Egyptian Queen was one of the most successful in this project. Cleopatra, with the asp at her wrist, sits calmly in the midst of her drooping and fallen maids, serene and majestic in her death.

✳ W. Clark (d.1801), *Cleopatra*, engraving by Clark (London: John & Josiah Boydell, March 25, 1790). Clark's version of Cleopatra appears more the saintly Roman martyr than the Egyptian Queen. The costume and setting are Italian, and Cleopatra's soulful gaze to heaven makes her look more like an early Christian saint than a seductive pagan queen.

✳ August Friedrich Spiess (1806–1855), *Antony and Cleopatra, Act V, scene ii,* engraving by W. Schmidt (N.p.: n.d.). Spiess was a German artist who specialized in historical and religious topics. Like Damer, he shows Cleopatra with her two maids at the moment of death. She is serene, as in Damer's picture, but beyond that, Spiess has made her languid and sensuous. Spiess's countryman, Heinrich Heine, remarked, "Cleopatra is—a woman. She loves and betrays at the same time . . . my old teacher was quite right—it *is* utterly dangerous to enter into intimate relations with such a person as Cleopatra."

Turning the Century

*

THE EXHIBITION, PART IV

*

Georgianna Ziegler

* Ellen Terry (1847–1928), *Four Lectures on Shakespeare*. Edited with an Introduction by Christopher St. John (London: Martin Hopkinson Ltd., 1932).

Ellen Terry's fame as an English actress at the end of the nineteenth century was equaled earlier in the century by that of Sarah Siddons. Terry brought great intelligence and wit to the many roles she created with her leading man and manager, Sir Henry Irving. She gave this series of four lectures from 1911–1921 in a variety of places from New Zealand to America. Two lectures deal specifically with the heroines: "The Triumphant Women" (including Beatrice, Portia, and Rosalind) and "The Pathetic Women" (including Viola, Desdemona, Juliet, Lady Macbeth). In the former she writes: "Wonderful women! Have you ever thought how much

we all, and women especially, owe to Shakespeare for his vindication of woman in these fearless, high-spirited, resolute and intelligent heroines?" She continues by suggesting that these heroines owe much "to the liberal ideas about sex which were fermenting in Shakespeare's age. The assumption that 'the woman's movement' is of very recent date—something peculiarly modern—is not warranted by history." The editor, Christopher St. John, was Terry's daughter, Edith Craig.

* Giuseppe Cosentino (b.1852), *Le Donne Di Shakespeare: Desdemona* (Bologna: Presso La Libreria Treves di Luigi Beltrami, 1906). Cosentino wrote several works on Shakespeare, including this essay on Desdemona and one on Ophelia in a series on the heroines. The advertisement suggests that the author intended to

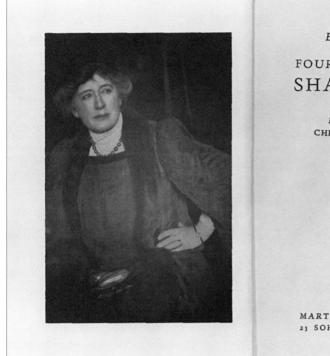

ELLEN TERRY

FOUR LECTURES ON

SHAKESPEARE

Edited with an Introduction by
CHRISTOPHER ST. JOHN

MARTIN HOPKINSON LTD
23 SOHO SQUARE LONDON

Ellen Terry (1847–1928), Four Lectures on Shakespeare.
Edited with an Introduction by Christopher St. John (Edith Craig)
(London: Martin Hopkinson Ltd., 1932).

write "uno studio psicologico interno alle donne delle tragedie shakespeariane," which puts his work in the context of other psychoanalytical studies such as those of Coriat and Harris that were becoming popular at the turn of the century.

✳ Julia Hall Bartholomew, "Women of Shakespeare," in *Two Masques* (Boston: The Gorham Press, 1916). This is one of many pieces written for the commemoration of the three-hundredth anniversary of Shakespeare's death in 1916. The masque opens with an address by Shakespeare "before Queen Elizabeth and her court ladies." Acting as Presenter, Shakespeare introduces the masque which brings female characters from the comedies, histories, tragedies, and classical plays before the Queen.

✳ Théodore Maurer (b.1873), *Les Femmes de Shakespeare* (Paris: En la Maison des Poètes, 1901). Maurer's collection presents twenty-six sonnets, each one on a different heroine. In the sonnet on "Lady Macbeth," he evokes her thoughts during the sleepwalking scene. The last stanza reads:
Des flambeaux! apportez des flambeaux! apportez
Des torches! . . . Sous mes yeux, de terreur dilatés,
La tache sur ma main brûle comme un fer rouge!
Lights! Bring lights! bring torches! . . .
Under my eyes, dilated with terror,
The stain on my hand burns like a red fire!

✳ Isador H. Coriat, M.D. (1875–1943), *The Hysteria of Lady Macbeth* (New York: Moffat, Yard and Company, 1912). Coriat was a Boston psychoanalyst in the early days of that branch of medicine; he knew William James and came to accept Freud only after some misgivings. Coriat wrote several books for a popular audience, including this one which is dedicated to his wife, the daughter of a rabbi. In it he discusses somnambulism, or sleepwalking, which he says Shakespeare shows in Lady Macbeth "with a startling degree of accuracy." "She is not the victim of a blind fate or destiny or punished by a moral law," he concludes, "but affected by a mental disease."

✳ James Thomas ('Frank') Harris (1856–1931), *The Women of Shakespeare* (London: Methuen & Co., 1911). Harris was a prolific British journalist, writer of short stories, biography, and autobiography and a self-promoter who knew Oscar Wilde. He sees this book as complementary to his earlier work, *The Man Shakespeare* (1909). "I had thought of calling it *The Woman Shakespeare*," he says, "for the woman a man loves is the ideal in himself," but he changed the title "in order also to mention and describe all the women who in any conspicuous degree entered into the poet's life and affected his art." Harris's approach may be judged from his conflation of the woman he believes was the love of Shakespeare's life, the maid of honor Mary Fitton, and the woman Shakespeare created near the end of his career, Cleopatra. His writing and Coriat's reflect a new popularizing of Shakespeare with a psychoanalytic approach.

✳ Anna Jameson (1794–1860), *Shakspeare's Heroines* (London: George Bell & Sons, 1897). Anna Jameson's *Characteristics of Women* was first published in 1832 and remained in print throughout the century.

Sixty-five years later this special edition of 175 copies appeared with colored plates showing famous actresses in the roles. The frontispiece reproduces the magnificent portrait of Ellen Terry as Lady Macbeth, painted by John Singer Sargent (1889). He depicts her as a commanding figure, holding the crown aloft with defiant pleasure in a moment we never see in the play. The costume was sewn over with beetle wings to make it look shiny and scale-like, thus creating an imposing Eve-serpent figure who gleams out of the half-twilight of the painting. She is the Lilith-figure, the temptress, who Nina Auerbach and Bram Dijkstra have shown both fascinated and frightened the mid- and late-nineteenth century.

✳ Supplement to *The New York Times*, Sunday, March 5, 1916. From February 20 to April 23, 1916, *The New York Times* published ten special supplements on Shakespeare with articles and poems by a number of well-known writers, critics, and actors, some written especially for the occasion of the three-hundredth anniversary of Shakespeare's death, others reprinted from earlier works. These articles were all the more remarkable for their appearance at the height of World War I, a conflict that the United States was soon to enter. "Even in a world shaken to its foundations by Titanic energies," Charlotte Stopes wrote in 1916, "we can turn to [Shakespeare] and gain from him new strength and courage, new heart and hope."

The articles on Shakespeare's heroines were contributed by two actresses, Viola Allen and Margaret Anglin, and by the early feminist, Charlotte Perkins Gilman. Those by Allen and Gilman in particular reflect the new thinking about the position of women in society that grew out of nineteenth-century movements for abolition and suffrage and soon precipitated new demands for womanpower to replace men in all aspects of society during the war. Their attitude is epitomized in Allen's title, "Seen as Modern Types, People of Today: Lady Macbeth a Politician's Wife, Rosalind the Alert, Up-to-Date Girl," and in Gilman's insistence that Shakespeare shows "not only the womanly virtues of these heroines, but their broad humanness, that preponderant quality to which we are still so generally oblivious." Moving beyond the moral characteristics that were gendered "feminine" in the nineteenth century, Gilman espouses qualities that are not gendered but belong to our nature as human beings.

Recent Critical Approaches to Shakespeare's Heroines

*

Frances E. Dolan

Miami University of Ohio

"Shakespeare's heroines," by which I mean the female protagonists in his plays, deferring, for now, the tricky question of exactly what it means to be a hero or heroine, meet a rather limited range of fates. In the comedies, for the most part, they marry, and the plots chart the courtships leading up to this consummation. These are generally considered happy endings, although a play such as *The Taming of the Shrew*, which sticks with the bride and groom after their wedding day, casts some doubt on that assumption. In the tragedies, for the most part, the female protagonists die; a few are murdered, but most commit suicide. It should be said, of course, that in the comedies and tragedies, the heroes meet roughly similar fates, marriage or death, although they tend to talk a great deal more on their way to the altar or the grave. In tragedies especially, because the male characters have more lines and more time on stage, we have more evidence about what they feel and what motivates them to act as they do. What is missing for female characters in Shakespearean tragedy, according to Linda Bamber, is "the sense of an identity discovering itself, judging and shaping itself"— the self consciousness and capacity for change that characterize the heroes.[1] In the romances, some of the younger female protagonists wend their way toward the comic destiny of marriage, while their mothers meet, then rebound from, the tragic destiny of death. In the histories, each of which is named after some king or other, the women play rather minor roles; as Phyllis Rackin has argued, the one role that no woman can play in a Shakespearean history is that of hero:

Aliens in the masculine world of history, women can threaten or validate the men's historical projects, but they can never take the center of history's stage or become the subjects

of its stories. Taking their subjects from patri-
archal history, Shakespeare's history plays
marginalize the roles of the wives and mothers,
centering instead on the heroic legacies of the
fathers, the failures and triumphs of the sons.[2]
To summarize, then, we might paraphrase
the mnemonic device used to help school-
children remember the fates of Henry the
VIII's wives—divorced, beheaded, died;
divorced, beheaded, survived—to outline in
crude terms the fates of Shakespeare's heroines in comedy, tragedy, romance, and history:
married, died, married, revived, marginalized.

The fortunes of Shakespeare's heroines
in twentieth-century criticism have been more
varied than in the plays themselves. As this
exhibit proves, the heroines have long been
popular on the stage and in the imaginations
of readers and viewers, even if the plays were,
in the eighteenth and nineteenth centuries,
available mostly in excerpted or altered versions. While women did not begin working
as critics and editors of the plays only in the
twentieth century, as the first essay demon-
strates, women's increased participation in
academic work, and the emergence of feminist
criticism, did combine to focus more attention
on the heroines than ever before. To emphasize the significance of women and feminism
in the twentieth-century study of Shakespeare's heroines is not to say that only feminist women are interested in women and
gender, that women only started to respond
to Shakespeare's plays in the twentieth century, or that women inevitably identify only
with the female characters they see before
them on the stage and screen. However,
twentieth-century critics, including many
more women, have paid more attention to
the heroines, and have articulated a broader
range of responses to them. Some have
joined in a long tradition of disparaging the
heroines, disappointed that they are not bet-

ter role models; others have reclaimed and
celebrated the heroines. These sharply
opposed attitudes toward the heroines often
correspond to sharply opposed attitudes
toward Shakespeare. Those critics who
express disappointment in the heroines for
not being strong, or vocal, or independent
enough, often also criticize Shakespeare for
his misogyny, conservatism, and failures of
imagination; those who insist on the spunk
and strength of various heroines often defend
Shakespeare in the process as a protofeminist.
In her groundbreaking book on *Shakespeare
and the Nature of Women* (1975), Juliet
Dusinberre, for instance, insists that "Shakespeare saw men and women as equal in a
world which declared them unequal"; in the
landmark anthology *The Woman's Part:
Feminist Criticism of Shakespeare* (1980),
Claire Claiborne Park remarks that "as
classics go, Shakespeare isn't bad reading
for a girl" largely because "Shakespeare
liked women and respected them."[3]

Much of the most interesting work lately
is moving beyond praise or blame for the
heroines, as well as beyond groundless spec-
ulation about how Shakespeare felt about
women, and tired debates over whether
Shakespeare was conservative or radical,
misogynist or feminist, in order to locate
Shakespeare, and his representations of
women in *his* cultural moment rather than
our own. While we still study Shakespeare
most often in isolation, as if he were the only
writer in sixteenth- and seventeenth-century
Britain, he did not, of course, write and pro-
duce his plays in a vacuum. Therefore, many
critics are working to reattach him to the
culture in which he participated. How do
Shakespeare's representations of love and
marriage, or of women, compare to others
available in his culture? How does he look
different when we compare him not only to

his sources which, as we know, he plagia-rized with abandon and creativity, but also to the works of his contemporaries, to the works of early women writers, to other equally pop-ular and accessible forms such as ballads and broadsides circulated in the streets, sermons, folktales, and jokes available even to the illiterate?

Such approaches qualify Hamlet's claim that drama holds a mirror up to nature by arguing, instead, that the drama does not have the distance from the culture it observes and depicts that this image implies. Rather, drama is a vital part of the debates and con-flicts which constitute a culture; it records or reflects these controversies, but it also participates in and even redirects them. Thus Shakespeare's heroines are increasingly being considered not only in relation to one another but on a spectrum of representations of women in the sixteenth and seventeenth centuries, a spectrum in which there are many other possible characterizations of shrews, queens, mothers, wives, etc. Much of this recent work is driven not by questions such as: Are the heroines role models for twentieth-century female readers and view-ers, or is Shakespeare a feminist? It is driven by the more basic questions of feminist inquiry: How does gender shape the charac-terizations of both women and men in these plays? What are the available options for representing women in Shakespeare's cul-ture? How does Shakespeare choose among those options, revising, recombining, expand-ing and inventing? What are the limits those options impose on the possibilities for imag-ining women as subjects, that is, as capable of self-conscious thought, of speech, and of responsible action, as the heroes are? What will we notice when we make women the focus of our attention, even if they are not the focus of the plays? For talking about

Shakespeare's heroines frequently requires a re-orientation, since in tragedy and history they are usually in the plays' peripheral vision.

We should not assume that female spec-tators or readers of the plays in the Renais-sance identified only with female characters, any more than they do now. Women were in the audience in English Renaissance play-houses; while we know little about their reactions to or interpretations of the drama, we know that they had access to it, and we can only guess that their responses were varied. The two most famous anecdotes about a woman's response to the drama regard Queen Elizabeth's identification with male characters. One story claims that six months after the performance of a dramatization of Richard II's history on the eve of the Essex rebellion, Elizabeth drew a disturbing connection between herself and the deposed and execut-ed monarch: "I am Richard II, know ye not that?"[4] The other story claims that Elizabeth so enjoyed the character of Falstaff in the *Henry IV* plays that she asked Shakespeare to resurrect him and depict him in love; he complied with *The Merry Wives of Windsor*. The Richard II story is widely discredited; the Falstaff story may also be apocryphal. What strikes me as important in these stories is not whether they are true, however, but that they have seemed worthy of repetition for centuries. In both, the queen identifies with a male protagonist; she does not, for instance, ask for a play in which Mistress Quickly is the star.

Perhaps this is not surprising, however, given that women in Renaissance audiences, not unlike women who go to most movies now, had to identify against gender if they wished to imagine themselves as characters who have a range of options, who make choices, who act decisively, who change the world and shape their own destinies. The place of the heroine in Shakespeare's plays is rarely at the center. In comedy and romance, female characters have far more substantial roles than they have in tragedy and history. In these genres, however, the heroines spar with their potential mates in heterosexual plots that work toward the subordination of wife to husband through marriage. These heroines, it has been argued, do not question or change the *status quo*; they merely secure for themselves the best possible situation within it. They often use male disguise to effect the arrangements they desire, reinforcing an association between masculinity and self-determination, but they discard male clothing and male privileges when they have secured their aims: marriage to the preferred man.

Comedy and, to a certain extent, romance are both organized around couples and communities rather than around individuals. Both genres focus on continuity, fertility, forgiveness. Tragedy, in contrast, is more concerned with the fatal mortality of each individual, with funerals rather than births and marriages, with the impossible struggle to forget or forgive. Thus Shakespeare's tragedies focus more sharply on a single figure and his internal and external conflicts than do the comedies or romances. They do not, however, place a female character in this anguished yet privileged spot. There is no female equivalent of Othello or Hamlet, commanding our attention as she explores her own feelings and motivations, making choices and taking actions that will affect others and shape the course of her own life and of the play. Instead, the female characters become subsidiaries, sometimes even the victims, of the heroes. In *Othello*, critics have argued, Desdemona dwindles as the play progresses; although she is at first capable of pursuing and asserting her desire for Othello, she progressively becomes less capable of defending herself or

averting, let alone reshaping, her destiny. Ophelia becomes so passive a figure that she submits to, rather than commits, suicide.

Even in a play like *Macbeth*, in which Lady Macbeth shares responsibility with her husband, she dies first, offstage, and he gets the long speeches and the big finish. No critic has suggested that the play might more properly be called *The Macbeths*. The female character with the strongest claim to being a tragic hero is certainly Cleopatra, who must share the spotlight with her consort, Antony. She does, however, outlive him by an act, as well as command her share of the scenes and lines. She also seems to exert a great deal of influence over how the action unfolds, thus contributing to the gender inversion so many critics find in the play. It's not just that Cleopatra put her "tires and mantles on him" while she "wore his sword Philippan"; she also influences his movements, whether he fights by land or sea, whether he retreats, and finally, when and how he dies. As comparison to other plays suggests, her position is that of the male hero, who is defined as much by his capacity for choice and action, a capacity often called "agency," as by his moral virtue. Yet, at least structurally, Cleopatra also resembles female tragic heroes who command center stage in plays by two of Shakespeare's contemporaries: Elizabeth Cary's *The Tragedy of Mariam*, which was published but not produced, and which has received a great deal of recent attention as the only original play written by a woman in the English Renaissance, and John Webster's *The Duchess of Malfi*. Both prove that it was possible for Renaissance playwrights other than Shakespeare to imagine a female tragic hero. Like *Antony and Cleopatra*, these plays focus on the female protagonist's conflicts with men, especially her struggles to achieve both independence and erotic and emotional fulfillment. In each play, one member of the central couple has been killed off by the end of Act IV, leaving Act V curiously desolate. In each case, it is the female hero, Mariam or the Duchess of Malfi, who dies early, in part because her heroism, in Mary Beth Rose's terms, is one of endurance rather than of action; these female tragic heroes earn our admiration through their capacity to endure suffering, rather than their propensity for public action.[5] (This is not, however, true of Cleopatra, who stoutly refuses to suffer.)

For critic A. C. Bradley, what made a character such as Desdemona a victim rather than a tragic hero was her passivity, a quality that Bradley associates with both virtue and femininity. As Bradley argues,

Desdemona is helplessly passive. She can do nothing whatever. She cannot retaliate even in speech; no, not even in silent feeling. And the chief reason of her helplessness only makes the sight of her suffering more exquisitely painful. She is helpless because her nature is infinitely sweet and her love absolute. . . . Desdemona's suffering is like that of the most loving of dumb creatures tortured without cause by the being he adores.[6]

For Bradley, then, Desdemona is not fully human, and certainly not adult; to confer responsibility and agency on her would also be to incriminate her. To be innocent and "infinitely sweet," she must also be "helplessly passive." Recent feminist criticism would challenge Bradley in a variety of ways, since this criticism is as diverse as the critics themselves: some find in the play the evidence that Desdemona is depicted as an adult woman with feelings, desires, and a voice— all of which are so threatening that they must be stifled; others compare the play to other representations of women as desiring subjects and effective agents, arguing that Bradley's association of passivity with virtue

and, thereby, of action with masculinity and, for women, guilt, is not idiosyncratic or anachronistic. Rather, Bradley reproduces and perpetuates the most limited and limiting Renaissance definitions of femininity and masculinity. For these critics, Desdemona's diminution in the course of the play marks her inability to sustain her robust engagement with life in a culture which associates female agency with sin. Finally, some critics concede Bradley's claim that Desdemona is, ultimately, passive but question whether this necessarily precludes her being heroic.[7] Might there be a heroism in suffering?

While I cannot here explain definitively what a hero is, I do want to stress that conceptions of heroism were not only multiple and debated in the sixteenth and seventeenth centuries but also gendered. For instance, military heroism was available, for the most part, only to men. Yet administrative and diplomatic skills were becoming increasingly important, perhaps more important than skill on the battlefield; Shakespeare registers this change in plays in which great generals like Othello and Antony are doomed, and in which military prowess is often relegated to a mourned past and represented by ghosts in armor. Furthermore, in a culture in which how-to manuals on the art of dying well were best sellers, and Foxe's *Actes and Monuments* (popularly known as the *Book of Martyrs*), with its graphic narratives and pictures of gruesome martyrdoms, rivaled the Bible as the most widely circulated and accessible book, the heroism of suffering and submitting was increasingly held up as an ideal for both men and women. Thus, a heroine may not need to act decisively in the public sphere to earn her title. As Mary Beth Rose has argued, a heroism of endurance was more available to women (and non-elite men) than a heroism of action. Discussions of

Shakespeare's heroines, as this exhibit attests, focus not only on the heroine as an admirable figure, or even an active one, but also on the heroine as a protagonist, who has more to tell us the more we question our assumptions about her.

The assumptions and expectations that shape our responses to the heroines change over time; as a consequence, different heroines, and varying versions of them, are popular at different times. The simpering submissiveness that one generation admires another finds annoying; one generation applauds a buxom Rosalind/Ganymede, whose sexuality is as sturdy as her figure and whose disguise conceals nothing and confuses no one, while another flocks to see an androgynous Ganymede. Most nineteenth-century critics would not have considered villains to be heroines, but recent critics and audiences have been particularly interested in characters such as Lady Macbeth, Regan and Goneril, and Cleopatra, who may be presented as sinister but who also, not coincidentally, have more substantial parts than their better-behaved sisters. Liberated from the obligation to defend and admire the heroines, critics are also exploring the way that the heroines share the limitations of the worlds the plays depict, and the ways in which they are as capable as male characters of abusing what power they possess. Miranda and Desdemona, for instance, share in racist assessments of Caliban and Othello; Kate beats servants and torments other women, although she quickly learns not to cuff her husband; Lady Capulet is no more sensitive to her daughter's plight than her husband is.[8]

There is additional interest in what the plays do *not* give us: the missing female characters, particularly the absent mothers in so many plays; the missing lines and speeches.[9] Where are the mothers in Shakespeare? Where are the female tragic heroes? Where are the heroines' soliloquies? Why are so many of Shakespeare's heroines silent at crucial moments? Why doesn't Kate have any lines responding to Petruchio's claim that they are going to marry? What are we to make of Olivia's silence at the end of *Twelfth Night*, when all the complications of identity and desire are explained? From one point of view, these questions may seem to participate in a venerable tradition of speculating about the heroines' obscured personal histories: Did Othello and Desdemona have time to have sex? Is Desdemona the type who would cheat eventually? How many children had Lady Macbeth? But we notice these absences and silences without correcting them. For the question is not where these missing lines, scenes, and characters are, but what it is about heroines that Renaissance dramatic forms, so mastered by Shakespeare, cannot quite accommodate? In what ways do female voices and interventions get in the way of plot development and complicate closure?

Finally, much recent scholarship has drawn our attention to how the conditions of Renaissance performance sharply limit the possibilities for representing women on the stage.[10] There were no female actors and no female playwrights working in English Renaissance theaters. What we find in the drama, then, are just men's fantasies of what women are like, performed by boys. Some critics go so far as to say that Renaissance drama has nothing to do with women at all, since they had little or no control over the means of its production and never represented themselves. Women sometimes took non-speaking parts in English court masques or worked as actresses on continental stages (as they would in England after the Restoration), but women were not wage-earning actors on the English Renaissance stage. Was this simply a theatrical convention, like that in ancient Greek drama, which audiences assumed and ignored, or should we be ever mindful of the significance of this transvestite drama when we read or restage or interpret the plays? What difference did it make that Shakespeare's heroines were boys? One thing is widely agreed: Renaissance audiences understood that gender was a performance, that femininity was a part one might play (and put aside) as much or more than an innate and unchanging identity determined by one's anatomy, long before contemporary theory articulated this insight in quite this way.

Shakespeare's plays are self-conscious about this: Cleopatra dreads seeing "some squeaking Cleopatra boy [her] greatness / I' the posture of a whore" (Act V, scene ii, 220–221); Hamlet comments that the boy who plays women's parts has grown taller and hopes that his voice hasn't broken yet (Act II, scene ii, 423–428). In the Induction to *The Taming of the Shrew*, the Lord teaches Bartholomew the page how to play a lady convincingly by submitting to a husband "with soft low tongue and lowly courtesy" and weeping (Ind. 1, 113). The Lord's instructions reveal that the "woman's gift" of tears can be faked: "An onion will do well for such a shift, / Which in a napkin being close conveyed / Shall in despite enforce a watery eye" (Ind. 125–127). Thus, before we meet Kate and Bianca, we have been shown how a boy learns to play a lady wife, just as Kate and Bianca do in the play.

What relation, then, do the heroines bear to "real" women in Shakespeare's England? Critics are increasingly asking this question by drawing attention to the theatrical, literary, and social conventions that shape their characterizations, by comparing the plays to other kinds of evidence about women's experiences, and by searching for rare glimpses of how women responded to the plays.[11] Yet critics are also insisting that, while the plays may not offer evidence of how women really acted or felt, they do offer compelling evidence of how men perceived and represented women, and of the options available for understanding and depicting gender in sixteenth- and seventeenth-century England. Furthermore, the plays offer a reminder that the meaning of gender changes over time and space and as it intersects with other categories such as class or race. Race inflects Othello's manhood and Cleopatra's femininity, for instance, and class differentiates Olivia from Maria and Viola, or Desdemona from Emilia. With all of their cross-dressing and gender-bending, the plays also open up to question the assumption that sexuality is always heterosexuality, and that Renaissance households were inevitably organized around heterosexual relations.[12] Recent work has shown that many of the heroines' most fully developed and tender relationships are with one another; and all relationships depicted in Shakespeare's plays were, at the level of Renaissance theatrical practice, among members of the same sex. That Shakespeare's plays are still so central to late twentieth-century Anglo-American culture suggests that we are still struggling with these constructions of gender and sexuality, working to understand and expand the possibilities for being heroic.

Notes

1 Linda Bamber, *Comic Women, Tragic Men: A Study of Gender and Genre in Shakespeare* (Stanford: Stanford University Press, 1982), 8.

2 Phyllis Rackin, *Stages of History: Shakespeare's English Chronicles* (Ithaca: Cornell University Press, 1990), 147.

3 Juliet Dusinberre, *Shakespeare and the Nature of Women* (London: MacMillan, 1975), 308; Claire Claiborne Park, "As We Like It: How a Girl Can Be Smart and Still Popular," in *The Woman's Part: Feminist Criticism of Shakespeare*, eds. Carolyn Ruth Swift Lenz, Gayle Greene, and Carol Thomas Neely (Urbana: University of Illinois Press, 1980), 101. For surveys of and reflections on feminist criticism of Shakespeare, see Lynda E. Boose, "The Family in Shakespeare Studies; or— Studies in the Family of Shakespeareans; or—The Politics of Politics," *Renaissance Quarterly* 40:4 (Winter 1987), 707–42; and Kathleen McLuskie, "The Patriarchal Bard: Feminist Criticism and Shakespeare: *King Lear* and *Measure for Measure*," in *Political Shakespeare: New Essays in Cultural Materialism*, ed. Jonathan Dollimore and Alan Sinfield (Ithaca: Cornell University Press, 1985), 88–108.

4 For the debate over the credibility of this story, a conversation that supposedly took place between the queen and William Lambarde, see J. Leeds Barroll, "A New History for Shakespeare and His Time," *Shakespeare Quarterly* 39:4 (1988), 441–64; and James R. Siemon, "'Word Itself against the Word': Close Reading after Voloshinov," in *Shakespeare Reread: The Texts in New Contexts*, ed. Russ McDonald (Ithaca: Cornell University Press, 1994), 226–58.

5 Mary Beth Rose, *The Expense of Spirit: Love and Sexuality in English Renaissance Drama* (Ithaca: Cornell University Press, 1988), chap. 3.

6 A. C. Bradley, *Shakespearean Tragedy* (New York: Meridian, 1904), 147. For recent, feminist reflections on this topic, see *Shakespearean Tragedy and Gender*, ed. Shirley Nelson Garner and Madelon Sprengnether (Bloomington and Indianapolis: Indiana University Press, 1996).

7 On Desdemona, see, for instance, Carol Thomas Neely, "Women and Men in *Othello*: What should such a fool / Do with so good a woman?" in *The Woman's Part*; Lena Cowen Orlin, *Private Matters and Public Culture in Post-Reformation England* (Ithaca: Cornell University Press, 1994), chap. 4; Rose, *Expense of Spirit*, chap. 3; and Peter Stallybrass, "Patriarchal Territories: The Body Enclosed," in *Rewriting the Renaissance: The Discourses of Sexual Difference in Early Modern Europe*, ed. Margaret W. Ferguson, Maureen Quilligan, and Nancy J. Vickers (Chicago: University of Chicago Press, 1986), 123–42.

8 On the complexity of the heroines' relation to race, for instance, see Kim F. Hall, *Things of Darkness: Economies of Race and Gender in Early Modern England* (Ithaca: Cornell University Press, 1995); Ania Loomba, *Gender, Race, and Renaissance Drama* (Manchester: Manchester University Press, 1989); and *Women, "Race," and Writing in the Early Modern Period*, ed. Margo Hendricks and Patricia Parker (London and New York: Routledge, 1994). On the heroines' violence, see Douglas Bruster, "Female-Female Eroticism and the Early Modern Stage," *Renaissance Drama* n.s. XXIV (1993), 1–32.

9 On absent mothers, for instance, see Janet Adelman, *Suffocating Mothers:*

Fantasies of Maternal Origin in Shakespeare's Plays, Hamlet *to* The Tempest (New York: Routledge, 1992); Coppelia Kahn, "The Absent Mother in *King Lear*," in *Rewriting the Renaissance*, 33–49; Stephen Orgel, "Prospero's Wife," in *Rewriting the Renaissance*, 50–64; and Mary Beth Rose, "Where Are the Mothers in Shakespeare? Options for Gender Representation in the English Renaissance," *Shakespeare Quarterly* 42:3 (1991), 291–314.

10 On women in the audience and boys on the stage, see Dympna C. Callaghan, "The Castrator's Song: Female Impersonation on the Early Modern Stage," *Journal of Medieval and Early Modern Studies* 26:2 (Spring, 1996), 321–53; Jean Howard, *The Stage and Social Struggle in Early Modern England* (London: Routledge, 1994); Stephen Orgel, *Impersonations: The Performance of Gender in Shakespeare's England* (Cambridge: Cambridge University Press, 1996); Michael Shapiro, *Gender in Play on the Shakespearean Stage: Boy Heroines and Female Pages* (Ann Arbor: University of Michigan Press, 1994); and Susan Zimmerman, ed., *Erotic Politics: Desire on the Renaissance Stage* (New York and London: Routledge, 1992).

11 For recent work comparing Shakespeare's representations of women to others available in his culture, see Catherine Belsey, *The Subject of Tragedy: Identity and Difference in Renaissance Drama* (London and New York: Methuen, 1985); Dympna Callaghan, *Woman and Gender in Renaissance Tragedy: A Study of* Othello, King Lear, The Duchess of Malfi, *and* The White Devil (Atlantic Highlands, N.J.: Humanities Press, 1989); Lisa Jardine, *Still Harping on Daughters: Women and Drama in the Age of Shakespeare* (Sussex: Harvester, 1983); Karen Newman, *Fashioning Femininity and English Renaissance Drama* (Chicago: University of Chicago Press, 1991); Valerie Wayne, ed., *The Matter of Difference: Materialist Feminist Shakespeare* (Ithaca: Cornell University Press, 1991); and Linda Woodbridge, *Women and the English Renaissance: Literature and the Nature of Womankind, 1540–1620* (Urbana: University of Illinois Press, 1984). For women's responses to Shakespeare, see *Cross-Cultural Performances: Differences in Women's Re-Visions of Shakespeare*, ed. Marianne Novy (Urbana: University of Illinois Press, 1993); and *Women's Revisions of Shakespeare: On the Responses of Dickinson, Woolf, Rich, H. D., George Eliot, and Others*, ed. Novy (Urbana: University of Illinois Press, 1990).

12 See Mario Di Gangi, "Queering the Shakespearean Family," *Shakespeare Quarterly* 47:3 (1996), 269–90; Jonathan Goldberg, *Sodometries: Renaissance Texts, Modern Sexualities* (Stanford: Stanford University Press, 1992); and Valerie Traub, "The (In)Significance of 'Lesbian' Desire in Early Modern England," in *Queering the Renaissance*, ed. Jonathan Goldberg (Durham: Duke University Press, 1994), 62–83.

Are Shakespeare's Women Unruly?

*

Jeanne Addison Roberts
American University

In an exhibition focused on unruly women, it may come as a surprise to find that there are so few images of women that look genuinely unruly. Juliets look young and beautiful; Cleopatras are regal (rulers, and therefore literally *ruly*) and seductive; Ophelias and Desdemonas elicit pathos; Portias are imposing; Rosalinds and Violas are appealingly androgynous; the Merry Wives are merry; Kate seems more a victim than a serious rebel; and even Lady Macbeth with her dripping dagger displays the wifely dignity of a queen to be rather than rebellion.

Analyses of early reactions to Shakespeare's women suggest that they were ignored, minimized, or judged simply by their degree of conformity to contemporary standards for female behavior. The detailed discussion of nineteenth-century approaches to the women reveals that they were, in fact, valued precisely because they were not unruly.

Queen Victoria's favorite plays certainly do not celebrate rebellious women. Like Elizabeth before her, Victoria may have focused on the men of the plays. In *Macbeth* and *King Lear* the "heroes" are male, and wicked women seem to meet their just rewards. In *King John*, *Richard II*, *Richard III*, and *Henry V*, women are virtually invisible and/or powerless. And the comedies, where independent women flourish, are notably absent. Only *The Winter's Tale* offers hope for the success of a moderately unruly woman. Even in our own time, when the women have been studied much more closely, and the word *unruly* sometimes seems apt, a careful consideration of the cases suggests that Shakespeare's women are truly unruly only within well-defined limits.

The explanation for this seeming anomaly lies partly with actors and directors who, especially in the nineteenth century, may have thought unruliness unattractive and who wanted their leading ladies to arouse empathy and admiration rather than create role models for anarchy. But part of the responsibility lies with Shakespeare and his age.

Almost without exception Shakespeare's "unruly" women end up either ruled or dead. The great independent-minded female heroes of the comedies—Kate, Portia, Beatrice, Rosalind, and the Helena of *All's Well that Ends Well*—after exercising their powers subside happily into wives, presumably concurring with Portia's announcement when she agrees to be ruled by Bassanio and commits herself to "be directed/ As from her lord, her governor, her king," granting him control over her estate, her servants, and herself. Even the Amazon Hippolyta of *A Midsummer Night's Dream* and *Two Noble Kinsmen* succumbs willingly or unwillingly to marriage. By Elizabethan law all wives became the property and subjects of their husbands; and, although one may wonder whether Shakespeare's heroines will really become suddenly docile, the structure of the plays tells us that they will be ruled and that this is a happy ending. Modern audiences may still share the pleasure of this conclusion.

Even a married woman may, of course, occasionally be unruly, but the few married or widowed women who do not die are usually safely re-incorporated into the patriarchal structure in which they will be ruled. The discontented Adriana of *The Comedy of Errors*, sternly rebuked by the Abbess, seems to acquiesce quietly. The unruly Titania is confined once again to the hierarchy of her marriage, although not before she has her fling with an ass; and the two undutiful wives at the end of *The Taming of the Shrew* are at least discredited. Even the strong-minded Paulina of *The Winter's Tale* is safely provided in the end with a new spouse.

In many cases in the histories and tragedies the unruly are villains rather than heroes and predictably end up dead. Lady Macbeth is, of course, the prime example; but Gertrude of the dubious virtue in *Hamlet*, the ruthless Tamora of *Titus Andronicus*, the inhuman Goneril and Regan of *King Lear*, and the nameless wicked stepmother in *Cymbeline* also meet their just rewards. They are finally ruled by death. Juliet, Cordelia, Desdemona, and Cleopatra, though not villains, are at some point at odds with the established patriarchy and, like the villains, are terminally silenced. Queen Margaret in the history plays and the witches in *Macbeth* survive as shadows on the future and reminders that evil has not disappeared.

The exceptions to this pattern of marriage and death as controls on rebellion are both rare and intriguing. The most extraordinary exceptions are perhaps the Princess of France and her ladies in *Love's Labour's Lost* who reject, or at least postpone accepting, the proposals of their suitors and depart for home unwed. The undutiful Hermia in *A Midsummer Night's Dream* qualifies at least marginally because she succeeds in marrying the man of her choice in spite of her father's disapproval (she has a little help from the long-lasting magic which reunites her father's choice with his first love, Helena). The merry wives of Windsor, Mistress Page and Mistress Ford, and Anne, Page's daughter, are also unruly in their fashion. The wives make a fool of Falstaff and of Mrs. Ford's husband. Anne circumvents the marriage plans of both her mother and her father when she gets the man of her choice. All end up happily reconciled and go home to "laugh [their] sport o'er by a country fire."

One thing that makes the three plays in which these women appear especially interesting is that all three are plays with no known sources. It would be pleasant to suppose that Shakespeare, unconfined by outside influences, felt free to celebrate unruly women unreservedly. A major impediment to the theory, however, is that *The Tempest* too is a play without a known source, and the unruly Sycorax is dead at the start while the relatively docile Miranda fits the more usual pattern of happily scheduled, paternally arranged, matrimony. If Shakespeare was ever a closet feminist, he returned to the party line at the end of his career.

The truly extraordinary thing about Shakespeare's women is that, in spite of the fact that he fits them ultimately into prevailing societal norms, we remember them as independent, distinctive, and almost infinitely varied characters. They sometimes achieve a prominence unusual in the drama of the time. Juliet has more lines than Romeo; Rosalind totally dominates *As You Like It*; and Cleopatra gets a whole act without Antony. Particularly in the plays of the 1590s, Shakespeare has permitted us a vision of women with minds of their own who know what they want and succeed in getting it. And they accomplish this miracle without antagonizing most audiences. The feat becomes especially intriguing when we remember that during much of this early period Shakespeare was the father only of two daughters (his son Hamnet died in 1596).

The father/daughter relations in these early plays are far from monolithic. They reflect some of the ambivalences of Shakespeare's age and still of our own. Juliet movingly and sympathetically defies her father but dies in consequence. Jessica in *The Merchant of Venice* repudiates her father and his religion and marries the man of her choice, while Portia resolves, at least pro-forma, to abide by her dead father's wishes. Both get what they want. Kate's father obviously prefers his younger daughter but still arranges Kate's marriage. Bianca tricks her father and achieves a dubious future. Celia rejects her father, but Rosalind is loyal to hers and both seem to marry happily. Beatrice and Viola have no fathers but still achieve their goals with a little help from friends and fortune.

It seems to me remarkable that these plays reflect so accurately what still seem to be the dilemmas of fathers and daughters. Daughters may be devoted to their fathers but still need to establish themselves in new relationships. Fathers, inevitably possessive about their daughters, must learn to let them go, whether they approve of their choices or not. And no matter how unsuitable the choices, the social structure behind Shakespeare's comic tradition continues to decree that consummation constitutes a happy ending. Later, in the tragedies, non-conformist daughters like Cordelia and Desdemona die, but so does a dutiful daughter like Ophelia.

It is striking and, I think, significant that all the truly unruly women in Shakespeare are in fact rulers. Lively young virgins have the power of bestowing their love and of witty dalliance with lovers; but rulers have political power over men. When they are women, their unruliness is dangerous. Only after 1600 (perhaps because of the declining power of Elizabeth as Queen) do the ghosts of the powerfully villainous Queens Tamora of *Titus Andronicus* and Margaret of *Henry VI* and *Richard III* resurface in the forms of Gertrude in *Hamlet*, Lady Macbeth, King Lear's daughters, Goneril and Regan, the nameless Queen of *Cymbeline* and possibly Cleopatra. All come to bad ends. Shakespeare's greatest unruly female ruler, the African Queen Cleopatra, achieves both her lover and the love of audiences. The price is death; but she stage-manages her death and it is a glorious ceremony which occupies the entire fifth act of her play. She becomes a tantalizing vision of a woman who almost succeeds in conquering the curse on women with real political power.

Modern productions have made efforts to emphasize and even increase the independence and power of Shakespeare's women. Katherine, at the end of *The Taming of the Shrew*, on some stages speaks her praise of docile wives as a joke; and, in the Zeffirelli film, even Elizabeth Taylor, who reads the lines straight, inevitably evokes an ambiguous response in audiences quite aware that she is not only Kate but also Elizabeth Taylor, neither a docile wife nor a daughter in need of a dowry.

In *A Midsummer Night's Dream*, the Amazon Hippolyta often now signals her solidarity with Hermia, the rebellious daughter, and the daughter may remain unreconciled to her father but happy in her match in spite of that fact. In the same play, Titania's lines of capitulation to her husband after her interlude with Bottom are sometimes cut, as are Portia's lines giving her estate and herself to Bassanio in *The Merchant of Venice*. Rosalind in *As You Like It*, Helena in *All's Well that Ends Well*, and Paulina in *The Winter's Tale* are recognized as being in charge of much of the action of their plays. And the novice would-be nun, Isabella, at the end of *Measure for Measure* responds noncommittally, or even negatively, to the Duke's offer of marriage. But these are rather minor modifications. We may tamper with the texts or expand stage interpretation, but the plays continue to control non-conforming women.

More daring experiments in the empowerment of women in productions of Shakespeare have come in the form of casting women in roles scripted for men. Just in the Washington area the examples are notable.

In recent years the Shakepeare Theatre has cast a woman as a male Falstaff in *The Merry Wives of Windsor* and as the title character in Ben Jonson's *Volpone*. Even more adventurously, directors have changed male roles to female roles played by women as women. The Washington Shakespeare Company gave us Queen Lear and a female Banquo. George Washington University imagined a female Hamlet; and St. Mary's College, in the most radical transformation, produced a *Julius Caesar* with Antonia for Antony, Cassia for Cassius, and Octavia for Octavius. Such experiments are wonderfully illuminating and challenging of our stereotypical expectations in regard to gender, and they provide much-needed opportunities for female Shakespearean actors. But we need to remember that none of these efforts can finally turn an early modern playwright into a twentieth-century feminist. We should perhaps cultivate a sensitivity to Shakespeare's foreignness as well as to his lauded universality.

Suggested Reading

The following list focuses primarily on twentieth-century publications. It does not pretend to be exhaustive, but its purpose is to direct the interested reader to items that will suggest avenues for further exploration.

1. Biographies and Autobiographies

Altick, Richard. *The Cowden Clarkes*. London: Oxford University Press, 1948.

Auerbach, Nina. *Ellen Terry: Player in Her Time*. New York: W. W. Norton, 1987.

Coleman, Marion Moore. *Fair Rosalind: the American Career of Helena Modjeska*. Cheshire, Conn.: Cherry Hill Books, 1969.

Furnas, J. C. *Fanny Kemble: Leading Lady of the Nineteenth-Century Stage*. New York: The Dial Press, 1982.

Gold, Arthur and Robert Fizdale. *The Divine Sarah: A Life of Sarah Bernhardt*. New York: Knopf, 1991.

Kemble, Frances Ann. *Records of a Girlhood*. New York: H. Holt and Co., 1879.

_____. *Records of Later Life*. London: Richard Bentley and Son, 1882.

_____. *Further Records, 1848–1883*. London: Richard Bentley and Son, 1890.

Manvell, Roger. *Sarah Siddons: Portrait of an Actress*. London: Heinemann, 1970.

Martin, Sir Theodore. *Helena Faucit, Lady Martin*. Edinburgh: W. Blackwood and Sons, 1900.

Raby, Peter. *Fair Ophelia: A Life of Harriet Smithson Berlioz*. Cambridge and New York: Cambridge University Press, 1982.

Rowell, George. *Queen Victoria Goes to the Theatre*. London: Paul Elek, 1978.

Russell, Charles Edward. *Julia Marlowe, Her Life and Art*. New York and London: D. Appleton and Company, 1926.

Terry, Ellen. *The Story of My Life*. London, 1908. Reprint. New York: Schocken Books, 1982.

Tomalin, Claire. *Mrs. Jordan's Profession: the Story of a Great Actress and a Future King*. London: Viking, 1994.

Weintraub, Stanley. *Victoria*. New York: E. P. Dutton, 1988.

Winter, William. *Ada Rehan: A Study*. London and New York: Privately printed for A. Daly, 1891–1898.

2. Art and Literature

Altick, Richard. *Painting from Books: Art and Literature in Britain, 1760–1900*. Columbus: Ohio State University Press, 1985.

Ashton, Geoffrey. *Shakespeare's Heroines in the Nineteenth Century*. An exhibition catalogue. Buxton: Buxton Museum and Art Gallery, 1980.

Casteras, Susan P. *Images of Victorian Womanhood in English Art*. Rutherford: Fairleigh Dickinson University Press; London and Toronto: Associated University Presses, 1987.

Cowling, Mary. *The Artist as Anthropologist: The Representation of Type and Character in Victorian Art*. Cambridge and New York: Cambridge University Press, 1989.

Nunn, Pamela Gerrish. "Between Strong-Mindedness and Sentimentality: Women's Literary Painting." *Victorian Poetry*, 33 (1995), 425–447.

Pressly, William L. *A Catalogue of Paintings in the Folger Shakespeare Library*. New Haven and London: Yale University Press, 1993.

Reynolds, Kimberley and Nicola Humble. *Victorian Heroines: Representations of Femininity in Nineteenth-Century Literature and Art*. New York: New York University Press, 1993.

Roberts, Helene E. "Marriage, Redundancy or Sin: The Painter's View of Women in the First Twenty-Five Years of Victoria's Reign." In Vicinus, ed. *Suffer and Be Still*.

Ziegler, Georgianna. "Suppliant Women and Monumental Maidens: Shakespeare's Heroines in the Boydell Gallery." In Walter Pape and Frederick Burwick, eds. *The Boydell Shakespeare Gallery*. Bottrop: Peter Pomp, 1996.

3. Victorian Women

Anderson, Amanda. *Tainted Souls and Painted Faces: the Rhetoric of Fallenness in Victorian Culture*. Ithaca: Cornell University Press, 1993.

Auerbach, Nina. *Woman and the Demon: The Life of a Victorian Myth*. Cambridge: Harvard University Press, 1982.

Beetham, Margaret. *A Magazine of Her Own? Domesticity and Desire in the Woman's Magazine, 1800–1914*. London and New York: Routledge, 1996.

Bronfen, Elisabeth. *Over Her Dead Body: Death, Femininity and the Aesthetic*. New York: Routledge, 1992.

Dijkstra, Bram. *Idols of Perversity: Fantasies of Feminine Evil in Fin-de-Siècle Culture*. New York and Oxford: Oxford University Press, 1986.

Donohue, Joseph. "Women in the Victorian Theatre: Images, Illusions, Realities." In Laurence Senelick, ed. *Gender in Performance: the Presentation of Difference in the Performing Arts*. Hanover: University Press of New England, 1992.

Flint, Kate. *The Woman Reader, 1837–1914*. Oxford: Clarendon Press, 1993.

Langland, Elizabeth. *Nobody's Angels: Middle-class Women and Domestic Ideology in Victorian Culture*. Ithaca: Cornell University Press, 1995.

Loeb, Lori Anne. *Consuming Angels: Advertising and Victorian Women*. New York and Oxford: Oxford University Press, 1994.

Nead, Lynda. *Myths of Sexuality: Representations of Women in Victorian Britain*. Oxford: Basil Blackwell, 1988.

Rowell, George. *The Victorian Theatre, 1792–1914: a Survey*. 2d ed. Cambridge: Cambridge University Press, 1978.

Vicinus, Martha, ed. *Suffer and Be Still: Women in the Victorian Age*. Bloomington: Indiana University Press, 1972.

_____, ed. *A Widening Sphere: Changing Roles of Victorian Women*. Bloomington: Indiana University Press, 1977.

4. Women and Shakespeare

Since the publication of Juliet Dusinberre's seminal work in 1975, so much has been written on women and Shakespeare that this list can only be highly selective, focusing mainly on book-length studies. Interested readers will find more references in the notes and bibliographies to these books. Also included are a few nineteenth-century works, several available in modern reprints.

Adelman, Janet. *Suffocating Mothers: Fantasies of Maternal Origin in Shakespeare's Plays,* Hamlet *to* The Tempest. New York and London: Routledge, 1992.

Bamber, Linda. *Comic Women, Tragic Men: A Study of Gender and Genre in Shakespeare*. Stanford: Stanford University Press, 1982.

Barker, Deborah E. and Ivo Kamps, eds. *Shakespeare and Gender: A History*. London and New York: Verso, 1995.

Callaghan, Dympna C., Lorraine R. Helms, and Jyotsna Singh, eds. *The Weyward Sisters: Shakespeare and Feminist Politics*. Oxford and Cambridge, Mass.: Basil Blackwell, 1994.

Clarke, Mary Cowden. *The Girlhood of Shakespeare's Heroines*. London, 1850–51. Reprint. New York: AMS Press, 1974.

Dash, Irene G. *Wooing, Wedding, and Power: Women in Shakespeare's Plays*. New York: Columbia University Press, 1981.

Dolan, Frances E. *Dangerous Familiars: Representations of Domestic Crime in England, 1550–1700*. Ithaca: Cornell University Press, 1994.

_____. ed. *The Taming of the Shrew: Texts and Contexts*. Boston and New York: Bedford Books of St. Martin's Press, 1996.

Dowden, Edward. *Shakspere: A Critical Study of His Mind and Art*. London: H. S. King & Co., 1875.

Dusinberre, Juliet. *Shakespeare and the Nature of Women*. London: Macmillan, 1975; 2d ed. New York: St. Martin's Press, 1996.

Erickson, Peter. *Rewriting Shakespeare, Rewriting Ourselves*. Berkeley: University of California Press, 1991.

French, Marilyn. *Shakespeare's Division of Experience*. New York: Summit Books, 1981.

Garner, Shirley Nelson and Madelon Sprengnether, eds. *Shakespearean Tragedy and Gender.* Bloomington: Indiana University Press, 1996.

Gay, Penny. *As She Likes It: Shakespeare's Unruly Women*. London and New York: Routledge, 1994.

Hamer, Mary. *Signs of Cleopatra: History, Politics, Representation*. London and New York: Routledge, 1993.

Heine, Heinrich. *Shakespeare's Maidens and Women* in *Florentine Nights*. The Works of Heinrich Heine. Trans. Charles Godfrey Leland. New York: John W. Lovell Co., 1891.

Howard, Jean E. *The Stage and Social Struggle in Early Modern England*. London and New York: Routledge, 1994.

Howard, Jean E. and Marion F. O'Connor, eds. *Shakespeare Reproduced: The Text in History and Ideology*. New York and London: Methuen, 1987.

Jameson, Anna. *Shakespeare's Heroines*. 2d ed. London, 1889. New York: AMS Press, 1967.

Jardine, Lisa. *Still Harping on Daughters: Women and Drama in the Age of Shakespeare*. Brighton, Sussex: The Harvester Press, 1983; 2d rev. ed., 1989.

Leigh Noel, M[adeleine]. *Lady Macbeth: A Study*. London: Wyman & Son, 1884.

Lenz, Carolyn Ruth Swift, Gayle Greene and Carol Thomas Neely, eds. *The Woman's Part: Feminist Criticism of Shakespeare*. Urbana, Chicago, London: University of Illinois Press, 1980.

Neely, Carol Thomas. *Broken Nuptials in Shakespeare's Plays*. New Haven and London: Yale University Press, 1985.

Novy, Marianne, ed. *Cross-Cultural Performances: Differences in Women's Re-Visions of Shakespeare*. Urbana and Chicago: University of Illinois Press, 1993.

_____. *Engaging with Shakespeare: Responses of George Eliot and Other Women Novelists*. Athens and London: The University of Georgia Press, 1994.

_____, ed. *Women's Re-Visions of Shakespeare: On the Responses of Dickinson, Woolf, Rich, H.D., George Eliot, and Others*. Urbana and Chicago: University of Illinois Press, 1990.

Pitt, Angela. *Shakespeare's Women*. Newton Abbot, Devon: David & Charles, 1981.

Rackin, Phyllis. *Stages of History: Shakespeare's English Chronicles*. Ithaca: Cornell University Press, 1990.

Roberts, Jeanne Addison. *The Shakespearean Wild: Geography, Genus, and Gender*. Lincoln and London: University of Nebraska Press, 1991.

Rutter, Carol. *Clamorous Voices: Shakespeare's Women Today*. New York: Routledge, 1989.

Shattuck, Charles H. *Shakespeare on the American Stage: From Booth and Barrett to Sothern and Marlowe*. Vol. 2. Washington: Folger Shakespeare Library; London and Toronto: Associated University Presses, 1987.

Traub, Valerie. *Desire and Anxiety: Circulations of Sexuality in Shakespearean Drama*. London and New York: Routledge, 1992.

Wayne, Valerie, ed. *The Matter of Difference: Materialist Feminist Criticism of Shakespeare*. Ithaca: Cornell University Press, 1991.

Design by Antonio Alcalá and Wendy Schleicher
Studio A, Alexandria, Virginia

Printing by Hagerstown Bookbinding & Printing Company
Hagerstown, Maryland

Typeset in New Century Schoolbook and Bauer Bodoni

Printed on Mohawk Options